THE CYBERSECURITY WORKFORCE OF TOMORROW

The Future of Work

The future of work is a vital contemporary area of debate both in business and management research and in wider social, political, and economic discourse. Globally relevant issues, including the aging workforce, rise of the gig economy, workplace automation, and changing forms of business ownership, are all regularly the subject of discussion in both academic research and the mainstream media, having wider professional and public policy implications.

The Future of Work series features books examining key issues or challenges in the modern workplace, synthesizing prior developments in critical thinking, alongside current practical challenges in order to interrogate possible future developments in the world of work.

Offering future research agendas and suggesting practical outcomes for today's and tomorrow's businesses and workforce, the books in this series present a powerful, challenging, and polemical analysis of a diverse range of subjects in their potential to address future challenges and possible new trajectories.

The series highlights what changes still need to be made to core areas of business practice and theory in order for them to be forward-facing, more representative, and able to fulfill the industrial challenges of the future.

OTHER TITLES IN THE SERIES

Careers: Thinking, Strategising and Prototyping
Ann M. Brewer

Algorithms, Blockchain and Cryptocurrency: Implications for the Future of the Workplace
Gavin Brown and Richard Whittle

HR Without People? Industrial Evolution in the Age of Automation, AI, and Machine Learning
Anthony R. Wheeler and Ronald M. Buckley

The Healthy Workforce: Enhancing Wellbeing and Productivity in the Workers of the Future
Stephen Bevan and Cary L. Cooper

Cooperatives at Work
George Cheney, Matt Noyes, Emi Do, Marcelo Vieta, Joseba Azkarraga and Charlie Michel

FORTHCOMING TITLES

Spending Without Thinking: The Future of Consumption
Richard Whittle

Inspiring Workplace Spirituality
Judi Neal

THE CYBERSECURITY WORKFORCE OF TOMORROW

BY

MICHAEL NIZICH
New York Institute of Technology, USA

United Kingdom – North America – Japan – India
Malaysia – China

Emerald Publishing Limited
Howard House, Wagon Lane, Bingley BD16 1WA, UK

First edition 2023

Reprints and permissions service
Contact: permissions@emeraldinsight.com

British Library Cataloguing in Publication Data
A catalogue record for this book is available from the British Library

ISBN: 978-1-80382-918-0 (Print)
ISBN: 978-1-80382-915-9 (Online)
ISBN: 978-1-80382-917-3 (Epub)

ISOQAR certified
Management System,
awarded to Emerald
for adherence to
Environmental
standard
ISO 14001:2004.

Certificate Number 1985
ISO 14001

INVESTOR IN PEOPLE

To my wife Cara and to my children, Thomas and Grace. An achievement like this is neither accomplished nor celebrated alone. Without your love, support, and motivation throughout the writing process, none of this would have been possible. Thank you. I love you all very much.

CONTENTS

LIST OF FIGURES

Chapter 5

LIST OF TABLES

Chapter 5

LIST OF ABBREVIATIONS OR ACRONYMS

A&A	Assessment and Authorization
ADP	Automated Data Processing
AES	Advanced Encryption Standard
AFC4A	Air Force C4 Agency
AFI	Air Force Instruction
AFIWC	Air Force Information Warfare Center
AFOSI	Air Force Office of Special Investigation
AFPD	Air Force Policy Directive
AIMS	Automated Infrastructure Management System
AIS	Automated Information Systems
AMIDS	Audit Monitoring and Intrusion Detection System
ANSI	American National Standards Institute
AO	Authorizing Official
AODR	Authorizing Official Designated Representative
ASD(C31)	Assistant Secretary of Defense for Command, Control, Communication and Intelligence
ASIMS	Automated Security Incident Measuring System
ASSIST	Automated System Security Incident Support Team
ATC	Authorization to Connect
ATD	Authorization Termination Date
ATM	Asynchronous Transfer Mode
ATO	Authorization to Operate
BIOS	Basic Input and Output System
BMA	Business Mission Area
C&A WG	Certification and Accreditation Working Group
C&A	Certification and Accreditation
C2	Command and Control
C2W	Command and Control Warfare

C4	Command, Control, Communications, and Computers
C4ISR	Command, Control, Communications, Computer, Intelligence, Surveillance and Reconnaissance
CA	Certification Authority
CAAP	Critical Asset Assurance Program
CAC	Common Access Card
CAL	Category Assurance List
CAP	Connection Approval Program
CC	Common Criteria
CCA	Clinger–Cohen Act
CCB	Configuration Control Board
CCI	Control Correlation Identifier
CD	Cross Domain
CDS	Cross-Domain Solution
CERT	Computer Emergency Response Team
CERT/CC	CERT/Coordination Center
CFR	Code of Federal Regulations
CI	Counterintelligence
CIAC	Computer Incident Advisory Capability
CIAO	Critical Infrastructure Assurance Office
CIO	Chief Information Officer
CIP	Critical Infrastructure Protection
CIPWG	Critical Infrastructure Protection Working Group
CIRT	Computer Incident Response Team
CISA	C4I Integration Support Activity
CITAC	Computer Investigation and Infrastructure Threat Assessment Center
CJCS	Chairman of the Joint Chiefs of Staff
CJCSI	Chairman, Joints Chiefs of Staff Instruction
CMDS	Computer Misuse Detection System
CMS	COMSEC Management System
CNA	Computer Network Attack
CNDSP	Computer Network Defense Service Provider
CNSS	Committee on National Security Systems
CNSSI	Committee on National Security Systems Instruction
CNSSP	Committee on National Security Systems Policy
COE	Common Operating Environment
COMSEC	Communications Security
CONOPS	Concept of Operations

COTS	Commercial Off-the-Shelf
CSA	Computer Security Act
CSIR	Computer (and Network) Security Incident Response
CSS	Central Security Service
CSSO	Computer Systems Security Officers
CUI	Controlled Unclassified Information
DAA	Designated Approving Authority (DAA)
DARPA	Defense Advanced Research Projects Agency
DASD	Deputy Assistant Secretary of Defense
DASD(DT&E)	Deputy Assistant Secretary of Defense for Developmental Test & Eval
DATO	Denial of Authorization To Operate
DCI	Director of Central Intelligence
DCID	Director of Central Intelligence Directive
DCMO	Deputy Chief Management Office
DCPDS	Defense Civilian Personnel Data System
DES	Digital Encryption Standard
DIA	Defense Intelligence Agency
DIACAP	DoD Information Assurance Certification and Accreditation Process
DIACCS	Defense IA Command and Control System
DIAMOND	Defense Intrusion Analysis & Monitoring Desk
DIAP	Defense Information Assurance Program
DIB	Defense Industrial Base
DIDS	Distributed Intrusions Detection System
DII	Defense Information Infrastructure
DIMA	DoD Portion of the Intelligence Mission Area
DIRNSA	Director, National Security Agency
DISA	Defense Information Systems Agency
DISN	Defense Information System Network
DITPR	DoD Information Technology Portfolio Repository
DITSCAP	DoD IT Security Certification and Accreditation Process
DITSWG	Defense Information Technology Security Working Group
DMC	Defense MegaCenter
DMS	Defense Message System
DNI	Director of National Intelligence
DNS	Domain Name Servers
DoD CIO	DoD Chief Information Officer
DoD ISRMC	DoD Information Security Risk Management Committee

DoD   Department of Defense
DoDD   Department of Defense Directive
DoDI   DoD Instruction
DoDIIS   DoD Intelligence Information System
DODIN   Department of Defense Information Networks
DoDM   DoD Manual
DoE   Department of Energy
DoN   Department of the Navy
DOT&E   Director, Operational Test and Evaluation
DREN   Defense Research and Engineering Network
DSAWG   Defense IA Security Accreditation Working
               Group
DSS   Defense Security Service
DT&E   Developmental Test and Evaluation
DTM   Directive-Type Memorandum
E/APL   Evaluated Approved Product
EAL   Evaluation Assurance Level
EFOIA   Electronic Freedom of Information Act
EIEMA   Enterprise Information Environment Mission
               Area
EITDR   Enterprise Information Technology Database
               Repository
eMASS   Enterprise Mission Assurance Support Service
EOP   Executive Office of the President
ETA   Education, Training and Awareness
ETAPWG   Education, Training, Awareness and Profes-
               sionalization Working Group
FIPSPUB   Federal Information Processing Standard
               Publication
FIRST   Forum of Incident Response and Security
               Teams
FISMA   Federal Information Security Management Act
FIWC   Fleet information Warfare Center
FN   Foreign National
FOIA   Freedom of information Act
FSO   Field Security Office
FTS   Federal Telecommunications Service
GAO   General Accounting Office
GCCS   Global Command and Control System
GCSS   Global Combat Support System
GIG   Global Information Grid
GMITS   Guidelines for the Management of IT Security
GOSC   Global Operations and Security Center
GOTS   Government Off-the-Shelf
GSA   General Services Administration

GSII	Government Services Information Infrastructure
HBSS	Host Based Security System
I&W	Indications and Warning
IA	Information Assurance
IAD	Information Assurance Document
IAG	Information Assurance Group
IAM	Information Assurance Manager
IAO	Information Assurance Officer
IAPWG	Information Assurance Policy Working Group
IASE	Information Assurance Support Environment
IATAC	Information Assurance Technology Analysis Center
IATC	Interim Authority to Connect
IATO	Interim Authority to Operate
IATT	Interim Authority to Test
IAVA	Information Assurance Vulnerability Alert
IC	Intelligence Community
IEEE	Institute for Electrical and Electronics Engineers
INFOCONs	Information Operations Conditions
INFOSEC	Information Systems Security
INFOSYS	Information Systems
IO	Information Operations
IP	Internet Protocol
IPMO	INFOSEC Program Management Office
IPR	Internet Protocol Router
IPSec	Internet Protocol Security
IPTF	Infrastructure Protection Task Force
IRC	INFOSEC Research Council
IRM	Information Resource Management
IRS	Incident Reporting Structure
IRT	Incident Response Team
IS	Information System
ISO	International Organization for Standardization
ISRMC	Information Security Risk Management Committee
ISSM	Information System Security Manager
ISSO	Information System Security Officer
IT	Information Technology
ITMRA	Information Technology Management Reform Act
IW	Information Warfare
IW-D	Information Warfare – Defensive
JCCC	Joint Communications Control Center

JCIDS	Joint Capabilities Integration and Development System
JDIICS	Joint DII Control Systems
JID	Joint Intrusion Detection
JIE	Joint Information Environment
JIEO	Joint Interoperability Engineering Organization
JIWG	Joint IA Operations Working Group
JPO STC	Joint Program Office for Special Technical Countermeasures
JTF-CNO	Joint Task Force – Computer Network Operations
JWICS	Joint Worldwide Intelligence Communications System
JWID	Joint Warrior Interoperability Demonstration
KMI	Key Management Infrastructure
KS	Knowledge Service
LE	Law Enforcement
LE/CI	Law Enforcement and Counterintelligence
LEA	Law Enforcement Agency
MA	Mission Area
MCDES	Malicious Code Detection and Eradication System
MLS WG	Multilevel Security Working Group
MOA	Memorandum of Agreement
MOU	Memorandum of Understanding
NA	Not Applicable
NACIC	National Counterintelligence Center
NC	Non-Compliant
NCIS	Naval Criminal Investigative Service
NCSC	National Computer Security Center
NDU	National Defense University
NIAC	National Infrastructure Assurance Council
NID	Network Intrusion Detector
NII	National Information Infrastructure
NIPC	National Infrastructure Protection Center
NIPRNet	Non-Classified Internet Protocol Router Network
NISP	National Industrial Security Program
NIST	National Institute of Standards and Technology
NITB	National INFOSEC Technical baseline
NOC	Network Operating Centers
NOSC	Network Operation Security Center

NS/EP	National Security and Emergency Preparedness
NSA	National Security Agency
NSD	National Security Directive
NSIRC	National Security Incident Response Center
NSOC	National Security Operations Center
NSS	National Security System
NSTAC	National Security Telecommunications Advisory Committee
NSTISSC	National Security Telecommunications and Information Systems Security Committee
NSTISSI	National Security Telecommunications and Information Systems Security Instruction
NSU	Non-Standard Usage
OASD(C3I)	Office of the Assistant Secretary of Defense (Command, Control, Communications, and Intelligence)
OIG DoD	Office of the Inspector General of the Department of Defense
OMB	Office of Management and Budget
OPSEC	Operations Security
ORNL	Oak Ridge National Laboratory
OSD	Office of the Secretary of Defense
OSD/JS	Office of the Secretary of Defense/Joint Staff
OT&E	Operational Test and Evaluation
OUSD(P)	Office of the Under Secretary of Defense (Policy)
PAO	Principal Authorizing Official
PCCIP	President's Commission on Critical Infrastructure Protection
PGP	Pretty Good Privacy
PIA	Privacy Impact Assessment
PII	Personally Identifiable Information
PIN	Personal Identification Number
PIT	Platform Information Technology
PKI	Public Key Infrastructure
PM	Program Manager
PM/SM	Program Manager/System Manager
POA&M	Plan of Action and Milestones
POM	Program Objective Memorandum
PPP	Program Protection Plan
PPS	Internet Protocol Suite and Associated Ports
PPSM	Ports, Protocols, and Services Management
PPTP	Point-to-Point Tunneling Protocol

RCERTs	Regional Computer Emergency Response Teams
RDT&E	Research, Development, Test and Evaluation
RMF	Risk Management Framework
ROSC	Regional Operations and Security Center
RT&E	Research, Test, and Evaluation
SABI WG	Secret and Below Interoperability Working Group
SABI	Secret and Below Interoperability
SAP	Special Access Program
SAPCO	SAP Central Office
SAR	Security Assessment Report
SATAN	Systems Administrators' Tool for Assessing Networks
SBU	Sensitive-But-Unclassified
SCA	Security Control Assessor
SCAO	SIPRNET Connection Approval Office
SCAP	Security Content Automation Protocol
SCCVI	Secure Configuration Compliance Validation Initiative
SCG	Security Configuration Guide
SCI	Sensitive Compartmented Information
SCRI	Secure Compliance Remediation Initiative
SECDEF	Secretary of Defense
SEI	Software Engineering Institute
SET	Secure Encrypted Transaction
SIO	Special Information Operations
SIPRNet	Secret Internet Protocol Router Network
SISO	Senior Information Security Officer
SITR	Secret Internet Protocol Router Network Information Technology Registry
SLA	Service-Level Agreement
SM	System Manager
SNAP	Systems/Networks Approval Process
SP	Special Publication
SPB	Security Policy Board
SRG	Security Requirements Guide
SSAA	Systems Security Authorization Agreement
SSE	System Security Engineering
STIGs	Security Technical Implementation Guides
T&E	Test and Evaluation
TAG	Technical Advisory Group
THREATCON	Threat Condition
TPM	Trusted Platform Module

TRANSEC	Transmission Security
TRMC	Test Resource Management Center
TSN	Trusted Systems and Networks
U.S.C.	United States Code
UC	Unified Capabilities
UCAO	Unclassified Connection Approval Office
UCDMO	Unified Cross Domain Management Office
UCMJ	Uniform Code of Military Justice
UR	User Representative
URL	Uniform Resource Locator (Universal Resource Locator)
USD(AT&L)	Under Secretary of Defense for Acquisition, Technology, and Logistics
USD(I)	Under Secretary of Defense for Intelligence
USD(P&R)	Under Secretary of Defense for Personnel and Readiness
USD(P)	Under Secretary of Defense for Policy
USSTRATCOM	United States Strategic Command
VAAP	Vulnerability and Assessment Program
VAS	Vulnerability Assessment System
VPN	Virtual Private Network
WMA	Warfighting Mission Area

ABOUT THE AUTHOR

Dr. Michael Nizich, PhD, CISSP, is the Director of the Entrepreneurship and Technology Innovation Center (ETIC) and an Adjunct Associate Professor of Computer Science and Cybersecurity at New York Institute of Technology. He has more than 20 years of professional industrial leadership experience in Information Technology and Cybersecurity in a variety of industries, including aviation, education, law enforcement, and biotechnology. Nizich has held IT and Security leadership positions in both private and publicly held companies, higher education institutions, and nonprofit organizations.

He has more than 15 years of college-level teaching experience at four different colleges and universities and holds a PhD in Information Science from Long Island University, a master's degree in Technology Systems Management from Stony Brook University, and a bachelor's degree in Computer Information Systems from Dowling College. Nizich also holds a Certified Information Systems Security Professional (CISSP) certificate from the International Information System Security Certification Consortium (ISC^2).

He additionally directs New York Tech's Center of Academic Excellence for Cybersecurity Education, designated by the U.S. Department of Homeland Security and the National Security Agency, is the recipient and principal investigator of several Department of Defense Cybersecurity grants, awardee of two NASA contracts for cybersecurity technologies, and has been interviewed and quoted in over 20 technology-related articles in leading publications including the *Communications of the ACM, CIO Review, Crain's New York, The Economist*, and *InfoSecurity Magazine* representing over 5 million readers. Dr. Nizich is a leader in the field of Information Technology and Cybersecurity, the Chair of the NY Metro ACM Chapter, Education Committee Chair and board member of ISC^2 Long Island, and serves on various industrial and institutional advisory boards in a technology role.

PREFACE

Cybersecurity continues to be one of the fastest growing and expanding fields and is yet again forecasted for near exponential growth in new hires, corporate and government investment, and corporate and government losses from preventable breaches. Yet, we still do not have a comprehensive and synergetic understanding of the cybersecurity ecosystem between industry and government security leaders, the cybersecurity workforce, the emerging cybersecurity workforce, educational institutions, and the human resources sector which still struggles with recruitment and retention of new cybersecurity talent.

It is for this reason that I decided to research and write this book. The purpose was to provide a single point of reference that would provide a variety of readers with an understanding of the current field of cybersecurity, the most probable future of the field based on current trends and an illustrative guide to understanding the relationships and interdependencies of the various components that make up the field. These components include the various technologies that make up cybersecurity, emerging technologies, current cybersecurity workforce, emerging cybersecurity workforce, educational institutions, and of course the organizations that require the security in the first place. Additionally, the criminal element and the driving forces of cybercrime are included in these components since they are the impetus for the entire movement.

This book incorporates several different approaches in its scaffolding that I felt worked well to bring everything together for the reader. The overall approach was to first perform and implement a literature review of over 100 articles, books, websites, and interviews from industry, government, and educational leaders in the field. Next was to include a series of expert opinions and scenario-based thought experiments in each chapter to help the reader to position themselves in one of the scenario roles and hear from experts in the field. I then include probabilistic descriptions of the future of cybersecurity based on the topics discussed in the chapter coupled with the current and forecasted trends. And finally, I included a library of resources for the reader, regardless of their roles, to quickly access during their cybersecurity journeys for whatever challenges they may encounter and at any level.

In summary, this book is not intended to make the reader a cybersecurity expert but is intended to provide the reader with a broad understanding of how the various components of the cybersecurity field work together, explain current trends that are occurring, and provide insights as to what the probabilistic future of cybersecurity and the workforce will be so the readers can get better prepared for the future, regardless of what their specific role in cybersecurity is now, or will be in the future.

ACKNOWLEDGMENTS

I would like to acknowledge the researchers and authors whose prior research and writing made this work possible, thank you all for allowing me to stand on the shoulders of giants. A special thank you to all of the cybersecurity experts in industry, academia, and government who were so accommodating during my research and finally, a special thank you to all at Emerald Publishing who believed in this work and the value that it will provide to individuals and organizations in government, industry, and academia as they help to build the cybersecurity workforce of tomorrow.

1

AN INTRODUCTION TO THE FIELD OF CYBERSECURITY AND THE CURRENT WORKFORCE GAP

INTRODUCTION

Throughout this book, there are numerous topics discussed in the area of cybersecurity including breaches, technology, data loss and prevention, and the cybersecurity workforce gap to name a few. However, to adequately place them in context to the future of cybersecurity as a field, as an industry, and most relevantly, with regards to the cybersecurity workforce of tomorrow, a brief but detailed look at the background and history of cybersecurity is imperative to fully grasp the relationships between the various components that comprise cybersecurity.

So what is cybersecurity? Cybersecurity can be defined as "the collection of tools, policies, security concepts, security safeguards, guidelines, risk management approaches, actions, training, best practices, assurance and technologies that can be used to protect the cyber environment and organization and user's assets" (ITU, 2008) or as "both about the insecurity created through cyberspace and about technical/non-technical practices of making it (more) secure" Dunn-Cavelty (2010). There are several different ways to look at cybersecurity and they are from the perspective of both protective measures and of threats to data and systems. Protective measures focus on the mechanisms that defend against unauthorized use, modification, or exploitation, while threats to data and systems focus on the determinants of a system breach and the consequences of a breach such as organizational losses.

Cyberattacks are commonly known to adversely affect the functionality of computer systems (Nye, 2018) and can be thought of as any outside attack that could compromise the security of an organization or a system inside the organization (Sharma, Gandhi, Mahoney, Sousan, & Zhu, 2010). Malicious cyberattacks are acts that are carried out with the intent of destroying data or documentation for the users (Wood, 2000) and cybersecurity threats can hugely impact organizations, assets, and the people involved (Von Solms & Van Niekerk, 2013).

There are a few different perspectives that can be taken when considering the cybersecurity workforce of tomorrow. These primarily include the cybersecurity student, the job seeker, the transitional worker, the advancing cybersecurity professional and the human resource professional. Each perspective has its own interests and concerns regarding the future of the cybersecurity workforce including, respectively, what do I need to learn to become a cybersecurity professional? How do I find a job in cybersecurity now and in the future? How do I prepare for the future and continue to advance my cyber career? And how do I continue to competitively attract, recruit, and retain cybersecurity professionals at my corporate, government, or nonprofit organization?

Unfortunately, there is one more perspective to be considered when discussing the cybersecurity workforce of tomorrow and that is from the perspective of the cybercriminal. If the methods and behaviors of cybercriminals are not considered, the edge will be lost in understanding what we need to do to prepare for the future since we will not know what mischief the criminal element is preparing for us. The criminal element, now in a very organized fashion, researches, tests, and prepares malicious attacks that compromise our valuable data, and their methods will become more advanced with the introduction of more advanced technologies. As cyber professionals use these advancements to protect systems, cybercriminals are using these advances to come up with new ways to bypass any obstacles implemented by those professionals responsible for protecting the systems.

THE COST OF CYBER CRIME

Billions of dollars are spent on Cybersecurity each year on a global scale (Koch, 2017). In 2015, it was predicted that about $75 billion had been used to fight cybercrime and that the global cybersecurity market is expected to expand to $170 billion by 2020 (Morgan, 2015) which has now surpassed even that estimate. According to the Ponemon Institute's 2019 Cost of a Data Breach Study (Ponemon, 2019), the average cost of a data breach in 2019 is $3.92 million (Koch, 2017), or stated otherwise, $150 per lost or stolen record, a 1.6% increase from 2018.

Cybercrime and more specifically successful cyberattacks can cause devastating financial losses and negatively affect organizations and individuals as well. It's estimated that a data breach costs 8.19 million USD for the United States and 3.9 million USD on an average (IBM security report), and the annual cost to the global economy from cybercrime is 400 billion USD (Fischer, 2014). According to Juniper Research (Juniper Research, 2019), the number of records breached each year to nearly triple over the next five years. Thus, it's essential that organizations need to adopt and implement a strong cybersecurity approach to mitigate the loss. The national security of a country depends on the business, government, and individual citizens having access to applications and tools which are highly secure, and the capability of detecting and eliminating such cyber threats in a timely way. Therefore, to effectively identify various cyber incidents either previously seen or unseen, and intelligently protect the relevant systems from such cyberattacks, maintaining a highly skilled cybersecurity workforce is essential.

Several high-profile data breaches have occurred in recent years including the well-known breaches at companies like Facebook, Equifax, Exactis, and Under Armour. These incidents have renewed concerns about cybersecurity. In July 2017, Equifax's data breach affected over 143 million individuals, compromising such personal information as social security numbers, credit cards, drivers' licenses, dates of birth, phone numbers, and email addresses (Fleishman, 2018). Facebook's 2019 data breach similarly impacted 540 million records of individuals' personal information (Silverstein, 2019). Information from 340 businesses and individuals were affected by marketing firm Exactis' breach in June 2018 (Greenberg, 2018). The retail industry is not exempt, with Under Armour's May 2018 breach exposing 150 million customers' information. It is no longer a question of whether a data breach will occur, but rather when (Cheng & Walton, 2019), and understanding the attributes and contributing factors to maintaining a strong and effective cybersecurity workforce both now and in the future is imperative to the safety and well-being of all countries and people on a global level.

THE MARKET FOR STOLEN DATA

It is important to discuss an important driving force for the increase in both frequency and complexity of cyberattacks and that is the marketplace for stolen data. With any crime, specifically theft, there needs to be someone, commonly known in criminal justice, as a fence to sell the stolen goods to. In noncybercrimes, this is why we see burglars that only steal certain things from houses because they have someone that they know will buy it, buy it quickly and for a fair price. This is also why criminals develop modus operandis or MOs (methods of operation) which help us to identify them during our investigations. Similarly in the cyber world, criminals steal very specific data and their fences, instead of hanging out in a seedy bar in a dimly lit part of town, are hanging out on the dark web. The dark web is a network of specifically designed and generally untraceable websites and communications infrastructures for criminals to buy and sell stolen data. It is very difficult to, from a law enforcement perspective, locate, identify, and build solid cases against suspects operating on the dark web. It is even more difficult to prosecute criminals and to receive a guilty verdict from a jury of peers based on the sometimes broad and nonspecific body of evidence that can be acquired from system access logs and data retrieved from a home arrest based on a warrant.

Think of the dark web as the local shopping mall with stores and kiosks or the famous Marrakech markets, but instead of scarves and blue jeans, they are selling data, lots and lots of data. The dark web is the hidden collective of internet sites only accessible by a specialized web browser. It is used for keeping internet activity anonymous and private, which can be helpful in both legal and illegal applications. While some use it to evade government censorship, it has also been known to be utilized for highly illegal activity

(Kaspersky, 2022). However, the dark web comprises only a small portion of the entire internet while the rest comprises what is called the open web and the deep web. The open web is what we consider as visible to the public and makes up a very small percentage of web content. The deep web sits below the surface and accounts for approximately 90% of all websites. This portion of the web consists of things like company files, organizational databases, and internal intranets. An essential component of the dark web is browsers. Websites are hosted in an overlay network technology in the dark web, which is not accessible without special-purpose browsers like Tor (The Onion Router) or I2P (Invisible Internet Project) (Saleem et al., 2022). An example of a dark web network architecture can be seen in Fig. 1.

The dark web refers to sites that are not indexed and only accessible via specialized web browsers. The dark web, however, is a very concealed portion of the deep web that few will ever interact with or even see. One way to look at it is that the deep web covers everything under the surface that's still accessible with the right software, including the dark web, and this makes the dark web very attractive to criminals in that there is no webpage indexing by surface web search engines,

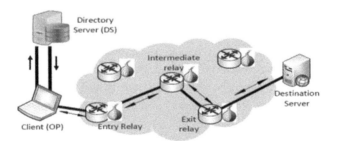

Source: Original diagram using Visio to create.

Fig. 1. Sample Dark Web Network Architecture.

there are virtual traffic tunnels that are only inaccessible by traditional browsers like Chrome or Firefox, and finally, it's further hidden by various network security measures like firewalls and encryption.

For the cybersecurity workforce of the future, professionals will need to be far more familiar with the workings of the dark web than they are required to be today. This not only includes a knowledge of the technical aspects of the dark web but also a willingness to work with law enforcement at city, state, and federal levels as there will be an increased push to identify and penalize cybersecurity offenders. As seen in the Solarium report, there is now a proposed structure to increase and intensify the law enforcement side of cybersecurity prosecution which means that cyber professionals will need to become more adept at identifying the details of the cybercrime from a criminal case perspective and not just a deterrence and recovery perspective. Currently, cyber professionals focus on working hard to deter any kind of attack and, if attacked, recovering quickly, efficiently, and affordably from that attack. Very few cybersecurity professionals today are focused on identifying the criminal, prosecuting the criminal, and stopping them from committing future cybercrimes.

CYBERATTACK METHODS

The modern computer network transfers data from one computer to another using a standardized process or protocol called the TCP/IP (Transmission Control Protocol/Internet Protocol) model. This process involves the deconstruction and reconstruction of information from simple binary values (0 or 1) that are represented as electrical signals over copper cables and Radio Frequency (RF) networks. These signals are then reconstructed into complex data representations that can be opened and accessed by advanced programs like Microsoft Word, Outlook, and so forth. Any cyberattack that manipulates these data between users in any of its states, such as a man-in-the-middle attack, or denies the ability of any one computer to contact any other computer, such as a denial of service attack, causes the network and its functional components such as switches, routers, and firewalls to operate as if they are at full capacity while they are really being underutilized at that time. In other words, the network breaks.

Like any common criminal, a cyberattacker has an MO in which they have a very specific crime that they commit and a very specific way in which they commit that crime. These MOs are usually geared around their ultimate criminal goal and their purpose for the attack. Some criminals are looking to profit financially from their exploits while others are seeking a change or alter some sort of political outcome. Whatever the reasoning is for the attack, these activities can all be considered malicious cyberattacks.

So what is a malicious cyberattack? A malicious cyberattack, if successful, allows unwanted access to unauthorized actors, resulting in potential loss of information integrity (Boyes, 2015). There are also nonmalicious acts that threaten the confidentiality, integrity, and availability of information within a system. For instance, if access is mistakenly granted to an unauthorized employee outside a project team, any intentional or unintentional change in the data leading to serious implications is counted as a cyber breach (Sommer & Brown, 2011). There are different forms of cyberattacks which might cause damage or disrupt the assets (Peng, Lu, Liu, Gao, Guo, & Xie, 2013). The different threats include intellectual property theft, degradation of assets, malware, viruses, worms, and spyware. It is critical to protect information security assets, both physical and virtual, against malicious attacks. Similar to physical assets in which they can provide protection to occupants against threats (Alguliyev, Imamverdiyev, & Sukhostat, 2018), IT infrastructure assets should also provide security to users against potential threats and attacks.

Cyberattacks can happen for many reasons and may be executed by many different types of attackers, each with very different goals and purposes. The type of cyberattack is not as important as the goals of the attacker. In other words, if an attacker has a goal of secretly recording keystrokes of a high-level government employee, there are several methods or attacks to achieve this, but the attack would not be considered disruptive or chaotic because nobody would know that it is happening. Conversely, if an attacker seeks to freeze production and functionality of an oil pipeline, then some of the same methods of attack can be used, but how they were used would result in absolute chaos, reduction in safety, and, quite possibly, the harming of innocent people and workers and even loss of life. A comprehensive list of currently known attacks may be found in Table 1.

There are also a wide variety of cyberattackers whose skill levels, purpose, MO, and reasoning for their malicious efforts are so different that there exists very specific names to refer to them so that cyber professionals have an idea of how to address each type of threat actor (Chapple et al., 2018). Table 2 contains the names and descriptions of these various threat actors.

THE CYBERSECURITY WORKFORCE GAP

The cybersecurity workforce of tomorrow faces an upward trend of an existing plaguing problem of a gap between the

---

Table 1. Types of Cybersecurity Attacks.

Methods of Attack

Malware

Phishing

Man-in-the-middle (MITM) attack

SQL injection

Zero-day exploit

DNS tunneling

Business Email Compromise (BEC)

Cryptojacking

Drive-by attack

Cross-site scripting (XSS) attacks

Password attack

Eavesdropping attack

Source: Original table – created from known documented attacks.

---

available positions for highly skilled cybersecurity professionals in industry, academia, and government and the
number of qualified candidates emerging on an annual basis
from two- and four-year institutions, professional development programs, and transitional workers moving from one
area of information technology or another into the field of
cybersecurity. As discussed earlier in this chapter, this gap is
currently estimated at between 1.8 million and 3.5 million
available positions (A Frost & Sullivan Executive Briefing,
2017). This gap is generally known and felt by industry and
government on a daily basis as they try to recruit and retain
new workers. To place these figures into some sort of context,
just imagine if these figures were shortages in healthcare

Table 2. Types of Cyber Threat Actors.

Types of Cyber Threat Actors

Recreational attackers	The main motive behind these types of attackers is fame and notoriety. They have limited resources and know which vulnerability to exploit for their cause.
Script kiddies	These are amateurs who learn from the internet and use available tools to crack a system. These noobs are harmless with less skill and do not cause heavy damage to the system. They enjoy being challenged and seek the thrill from it. Over time they may gain experience and even become professional hackers.
Cybercriminals	These attackers constitute an individual or a group of individuals whose aim is to exploit sensitive information of the user. They either capture the system or the data for financial gains. They undertake various approaches to achieve their purpose. Some of them are spreading viruses in a system, spamming the user with infected messages, or even stealing sensitive information of the user or a business.
Hacktivists	Hacktivists are those who perform malicious and fraudulent tasks to promote a political agenda. Hacktivism is a digital disobedience undertaken for a cause. Hacktivists fight for justice and do not go behind financial gains. Sometimes they pair up with malicious insiders to expose sensitive data.
State-sponsored attackers	State-sponsored attackers have specific goals associating with either the political or military origin of their country. They use

Table 2. (*Continued*)

Types of Cyber Threat Actors

	unlimited resources and highly sophisticated technologies. They often cause advanced persistent threats. Cyberwars, industrial espionage, and leaking state secrets are some of the attacks done by state-sponsored attackers.
Insider threats	Insiders come from within an organization and pose a threat to the security of valuable data the company holds. When the needs of the employee are dissatisfied they become disgruntled employees and eventually hackers. The insiders threaten the safety of the internal systems. These insiders may be financially motivated and some may even be unintentional. Former employees, temporary workers, or even customers may play the role of an insider. Insider attacks may be malicious, accidental, or negligent.
Organized crime	These occur due to the carelessness of an employee. This happens when an employee fails to follow the policies and procedures framed by an organization. The policies are put in place to protect the integrity of data and when not followed might accumulate to end up in a huge loss and open vulnerability for threats.
Hackers	Hackers possess the technical skills to breach the data by exploiting any vulnerability in the system or network. They have the skills to gain unauthorized access to your system. Hackers can be classified into three types based on their intent including white hat, gray hat, and black hat. White-hat hackers use

Table 2. (*Continued*)

Types of Cyber Threat Actors

	their skills in a just and lawful manner to determine the loose ends of the security of an organization. Gray-hat hackers test the security of an organization only to inform them later about it. They do not cause any harm but simply disclose the weakness in the security of the compromised network and black-hat hackers are unethical hackers who hack the system and networks and misuse it for personal benefits.
Nation-state actors or cyberterrorists	These attackers work in favor of the government and other vital businesses that run critical infrastructures for the society like power grids. They aim to steal highly sensitive information, damage the opponent's facilities, or launch an international incident. They work directly or indirectly for the government employing sophisticated attacking techniques against enemies. These attackers are patriots and work to put the nation in a better position by causing high-intensity damages to enemies.

Source: Original creation but some definitions sourced from: https://data-flair.training/blogs/most-common-types-of-cyber-attackers/.

workers, teachers, pilots, or farm and agricultural workers. What effect would that shortage have on us as a society?

This current shortage of skilled cybersecurity workers is an obvious critical factor for the future cybersecurity workforce of tomorrow. However, we are also now seeing the introduction of new and emerging technology skills beginning to be used in cybersecurity including the creation of machine learning (ML) algorithms, AI modeling, Internet of Things (IoT) software development, chaos engineering, and big data analytics that will inevitably become part of the future defense mechanisms against rapidly advancing cybercriminals. Because of this, it is possible that this gap will not only spread further but may cause a paradigm shift in human resource departments' approach to recruitment and retention efforts as the difficulty in finding and retaining cybersecurity talent may exceed the abilities of traditional human resource departments.

As cyber threats continue to grow in sophistication, organizations face a persistent challenge in recruiting skilled cybersecurity professionals capable of protecting their systems against the threat of malicious actors. With cybercriminals now responsible for billions in losses per year and state-sponsored hacking groups posing an ever-greater threat, the need for individuals capable of securing networks against attackers has never been greater. However, education and training institutions in the United States and around the world have so far found it difficult to keep pace with the growing need for cyber talent. As an example of this conundrum, a recent Center for Strategic and International Studies (CSIS) survey of IT decision-makers across eight countries found that 82% of employers report a shortage of cybersecurity skills, and 71% believe this talent gap causes direct and measurable damage to their organizations. According to CyberSeek, an initiative funded by the National Initiative for Cybersecurity Education (NICE), the United States faced a shortfall of almost 314,000 cybersecurity professionals as of January 2019. To put this in context, the country's total employed cybersecurity workforce is just 716,000 (Crumpler & Lewis, 2019).

Currently, shortages exist for almost every position within cybersecurity, but the needs for highly skilled technical employees lead the way and are in the highest demand. In 2010, the CSIS report, A Human Capital Crisis in Cybersecurity, found that the United States "not only has a shortage of the highly technically skilled people required to operate and support systems already deployed, but also an even more desperate shortage of people who can design secure systems, write safe computer code, and create the ever more sophisticated tools needed to prevent, detect, mitigate, and reconstitute from damage due to system failures and malicious acts" (Crumpler & Lewis, 2019). The International Information Systems Security Certification Consortium (ISC)[2] in a recent report places the overall global shortage at 4.07 million available positions. Fig. 2 shows the breakdown by region of this shortage.

Education providers are working to fill this gap, and full-fledged degree programs are rapidly emerging in this area. Industry training and certification programs have also been growing rapidly as well. But even with this growth, the gap is still expected to remain large, and the diversity of skills needed within this space is substantial. Multiple pathways are needed to prepare students to engage in different types of cybersecurity jobs. This topic is discussed in more detail in Chapter 5.

CHALLENGES TO GLOBAL BUSINESS AND GOVERNMENT

Unlike other industries such as healthcare, energy, or even finance where uniquenesses exist on a national level due to ultimate geographical borders or limits due to legalities, legislation or currency, or system incompatibilities,

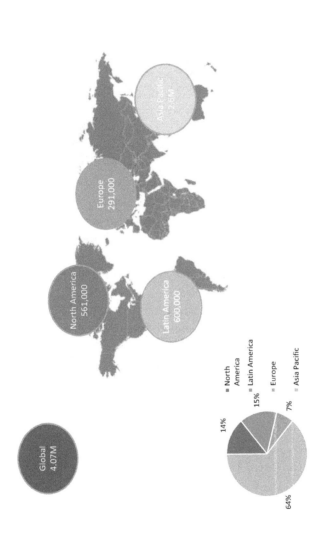

Source: Based on Brink news...https://www.brinknews.com/a-global-shortage-of-cybersecurity-professionals-leaves-businesses-at-risk/.

Fig. 2. ISC2 Cybersecurity Workforce Gap by Region.

cybersecurity is truly global. This is because a universal communication protocol or language is used for all devices that connect to the internet called TCP/IP. This means that every electronic device, regardless of manufacturer to geographic location, must speak the same language to communicate with other devices on the internet.

This presents a concern on a truly global level for data security but it also creates a global marketplace for skilled cybersecurity professionals making it even harder to compete for qualified candidates. The future of the cybersecurity workforce is not a national issue. It is a global issue and the presence of a global marketplace for stolen data combined with a global workforce sets the stage for a cybersecurity future that requires a broader and more robust model of management in order to recruit, train, retain, and manage a remote, international workforce of cybersecurity professionals and experts, who must be trusted at the highest level with the organizations' sensitive and valuable data. The cybersecurity workforce of tomorrow will be a global workforce and our security teams will be composed of workers from all back-grounds and nationalities so we will need to have systems and procedures in place for maintaining the highest level of ethics, trust, and privacy within our teams.

The current challenges to business and government, with regards to securing their valuable data, include selecting cybersecurity consulting companies, hiring full-time cyberse-curity employees, retaining cybersecurity employees, and embedding cybersecurity practices into their corporate culture and everyday business processes. 90% of executives cite skilled labor availability and quality as a critical factor for their organization when considering expansion into new markets. 54% of executives say cyber threats are among the biggest strategic risks for their nation's economy in the next five years. 120 million workers in the world's 12 largest economies may need to be retrained and reskilled in the next three years as a result of intelligent AI-enabled automation (Ikeda, Marshall, & Zaharchuk, 2019).

The cybersecurity workforce gap is a global issue and challenge. As in any labor shortage, the labor force is one of the most significant issues impacting national and regional economic vitality. Without adequate talent, public- and private-sector organizations struggle to effectively innovate, deliver value to citizens and shareholders, grow their businesses, and create new jobs. In the cybersecurity workforce gap, private-sector companies may be forced to seek out regions where they can obtain the necessary talent to remain competitive. Without adequate talent, regional economies struggle to retain and recruit industries that provide high-skilled and high-paying jobs. A decline in the quality of talent in regions can significantly impact the economic competitiveness and value proposition of the region.

Governments can take a leadership role in establishing policies that address growing cyber threats and establishing national cybersecurity strategies. As an international example, Singapore has established comprehensive national-level strategies with clear vision, goals, strategies, and priorities for cybersecurity. Singapore's national strategy enables coordinated action and facilitates international partnerships for a resilient and trusted cyber environment (Singapore's Cybersecurity Strategy, 2016). Addressing cyber threats also requires developing and maintaining skilled and trained cyber experts. Along with continued high demand for cybersecurity professionals, there is an ongoing shortage of talent as we have been discussing and organizations around the world are pursuing numerous ways to close the talent gap in both the short and long term, including new university programs, technical and vocational programs, apprenticeships, certifications, and early education and government programs. With cyber threats only expected to grow, educating and training the next generation of cyber experts will remain a critical initiative. The five pillars of the International Telecommunications Union (ITU) Global Cybersecurity Index can be found in Fig. 3 and Table 3.

Legal

- Cybercriminal Legislation
- Substantive Law
- Procedural Cybercriminal Law
- Cybersecurity Regulation

Technical

- National CIRT
- Government CIRT
- Sectional CIRT
- Standards for Organizations
- Standardization Body

Organizational

- Strategy
- Responsible Agency
- Cybersecurity Metrics

Capacity Building

- Public Awareness
- Professional Training
- National Education Programs
- Incentive Mechanisms
- Home Grown Industry

Cooperation

- Intra-State Cooperation
- Multilateral Agreements
- International For a
- Public-Private Partnerships
- Inter-Agency Partnerships

Source: Based on https://www.itu.int/en/ITU-D/Cybersecurity/Pages/global-cybersecurity-index.aspx.

Fig. 3. Five Pillars of the ITU Global Cybersecurity Index.

Table 3. The Five Pillars of the ITU Global Cybersecurity Index.

Global Security Index

1 Legal: Legal institutions and frameworks dealing with cybersecurity and cybercrime

2 Technical: Technical institutions and frameworks dealing with cybersecurity

3 Organizational: Policy coordination institutions and strategies for cybersecurity development at the national level.

4 Capacity building: Research and development, education and training programs, certified professionals, and public sector agencies fostering capacity building.

5 Cooperation: Partnerships, cooperative frameworks, and information-sharing networks.

Source: ITU Global Cybersecurity Index: https://www.itu.int/en/ITU-D/ Cybersecurity/Pages/global-cybersecurity-index.aspx.

MANAGING RISK

The cybersecurity workforce of tomorrow in some ways relies on risk. How much risk are organizations willing to take on based on the data that they are storing and the costs and efforts that they are willing to take on to protect that data. This is known as risk appetite and this measure of an organization, a nation, or even a global community's willingness to make only certain efforts to protect their data will have an enormous effect on the workforce of tomorrow. The reason for this is that if an organization simply puts in the minimal amount of effort and investment to actively secure their data and relies on system backups and disaster recovery plans as their primary source of security, then the cybersecurity workforce at that organization will be limited to only those workers that can perform those tasks. Conversely, if an organization considers the loss of data of any kind an unacceptable possibility, then their cybersecurity workforce will look much different.

In the domain of cybersecurity, organizations focus on risk. More specifically, how much risk they are willing to take to maximize their efficiency, productivity, and profitability through implementation of the latest technologies while securing their systems to the highest degree possible without compromising that performance. This is called their risk appetite. The cybersecurity workforce of tomorrow needs to be able to understand this risk appetite and be extremely open to taking risks that are manageable in order to provide the organization with the performance it desires and requires while at the same time implementing policies, procedures, and technologies to provide high levels of deterrence against a breach but also to assure that recovery from a breach is as painless as possible. This will require a combination of skill sets discussed in detail later in this text and will greatly affect the recruitment and retention process as well as the initial training process for cybersecurity professionals at the earliest stages.

Given the significant costs of a data breach to multiple parties, it is critical to plan relevant protection mechanisms in response to general and specific threats. Dewar (2014) notes that the optimal goal of cybersecurity is to enable operations in cyberspace free from significant cybersecurity risks (Walton, Wheeler, Zhang, & Zhao, 2021). Cybersecurity risk management is an ongoing process of identifying, analyzing, evaluating, and addressing your organization's cybersecurity threats. Cybersecurity risk management isn't simply the job of the security team; everyone in the organization has a role to play. Often siloed, employees and business unit leaders view risk management from their business function. Regrettably, they lack the holistic perspective necessary to address risk in a comprehensive and consistent manner.

So, who should own what part of security risk? The short answer is everyone shares full ownership and responsibility. Today's risk landscape requires a unified, coordinated, disciplined, and consistent management solution (Knaves, 2022). Table 4 displays key risk management action components that all organizations must keep in mind.

In order to manage an organization's risk, the cybersecurity workforce of tomorrow will need to be fully aware of the components and attributes of the National Institute of Standards and Technology's (NIST) Risk Management Framework (RMF) as it provides a comprehensive, flexible, repeatable, and measurable seven-step process that any

---

Table 4. Key Risk Management Action Components.

Risk Management Components

1 Development of robust policies and tools to assess vendor risk

2 Identification of emergent risks, such as new regulations with business impact

3 Identification of internal weaknesses such as lack of two-factor authentication

4 Mitigation of IT risks, possibly through training programs or new policies and internal controls

5 Testing of the overall security posture

6 Documentation of vendor risk management and security for regulatory examinations or to appease prospective customers

Source: NIST Risk Management Framework: https://csrc.nist.gov/projects/risk-management/about-rmf.

---

organization can use to manage information security and privacy risk for organizations and systems. It also links to a suite of NIST standards and guidelines to support implementation of risk management programs to meet the requirements of the Federal Information Security Modernization Act (FISMA).

RMF provides a process that integrates security, privacy, and cyber supply chain risk management activities into the system development life cycle. The risk-based approach to control selection and specification considers effectiveness, efficiency, and constraints due to applicable laws, directives, executive orders, policies, standards, or regulations (Fig. 4).

Source: https://csrc.nist.gov/projects/risk-management/about-rmf.

Fig. 4. NIST Risk Management Framework.

Managing organizational risk is paramount to effective information security and privacy programs; the RMF approach can be applied to new and legacy systems, any type of system or technology, and within any type of organization regardless of size or sector.

IT SECURITY GOVERNANCE: SECURITY STANDARDS, REGULATIONS, AND FRAMEWORKS

In any national or global system, there are frameworks that are used to assure that all individuals and organizations abide by certain protocols so that the system can function as normal with as little interaction between related parties and components as possible. Just as Institute of Electrical and Electronics Engineers (IEEE) has frameworks and protocols for designing electronics or the Federal Communications Commission (FCC) has frameworks for communication, cybersecurity has frameworks as well. We refer to this as governance. From a governance perspective, these frameworks are used to make sure that all organizations have a guideline to follow as far as what practices and controls should be implemented in certain situations to maximize the potential of a certain system being protected against malicious attacks. The cybersecurity workforce of the future will undoubtedly be utilizing these frameworks as they implement their security solutions; however these frameworks will also need to evolve to address some of the new emerging technologies that will be an integral part of future cybersecurity solutions and daily operations. In this section, we'll discuss the various frameworks in use today and in the future to help organizations and cybersecurity professionals properly secure their systems and data from threat actors and malicious attacks.

So what is an IT security framework? An IT security framework is a series of documented processes that define policies and procedures around the implementation and ongoing management of information security controls. These frameworks are a blueprint for managing risk and reducing vulnerabilities. Information security professionals use frameworks to define and prioritize the tasks required to manage enterprise security. Frameworks are also used to help prepare for compliance and other IT audits. Therefore, the framework must support specific requirements defined in the standard or regulation. Frameworks provide a starting point for establishing processes, policies, and administrative activities for information security management. Security requirements often overlap, which results in "crosswalks" that can be used to demonstrate compliance with different regulatory standards. Using a common framework, such as ISO 27002, an organization can establish crosswalks to demonstrate compliance with multiple regulations, including Health Insurance Portability and Accountability Act (HIPAA), Sarbanes–OxleyAct, Payment Card Industry Data Security Standard (PCI DSS), and Gramm–Leach–Bliley Act.

According to Walton et al. (2021), several guides and frameworks have emerged to address underlying cybersecurity risks and disclosures. In 2019, the Center for Internet Security (CIS) issued its CIS Controls Version 7.1 for developing and implementing cybersecurity controls, while in 2017, NIST issued a new cybersecurity control framework. In order to assist accountants engaged in examining and reporting on cybersecurity risks, the American Institute of Certified Public Accountants (AICPA) has also developed a cybersecurity risk management reporting framework (AICPA, 2017). Additionally, the Center for Audit Quality (CAQ) has published resources and tools to assist members of board of directors in identifying potential cybersecurity risks (CAQ, 2018). These processes of using frameworks to secure information systems are called IT governance practices.

Information security management encompasses many areas, from perimeter protection and encryption to application security and disaster recovery. IT security is made more challenging by compliance regulations, such as HIPAA, PCI DSS, Sarbanes–Oxley Act, and global standards, such as General Data Protection Regulation (GDPR) (Kirvan & Granneman, 2022). This is where IT security frameworks and standards can be helpful. Knowledge of regulations, standards, and frameworks are essential for all infosec and cybersecurity professionals. Compliance with these frameworks and standards is important from an audit perspective, too. It is important to keep in mind that these governance tools are in place because of an increasing level of loss, damage, and number of attacks each and every year. With the introduction and expansion of the use of emerging technologies like AI and ML into cybersecurity products and services, it is a given that these governance frameworks will continue to rapidly evolve to meet these needs and the cybersecurity workforce of tomorrow will need to adapt to these new frameworks.

Examples of IT Security Standards and Frameworks

There are several cybersecurity frameworks existing today that have become the accepted standards depending on what systems you are trying to protect. These frameworks include the ISO 27000 Series developed by the International Organization for Standardization, the NIST series of frameworks including SP 800-53 which has developed an extensive library of IT standards and ultimately led to the creation of the NIST Cybersecurity Framework (CSF), the COBIT framework created by ISACA, CIS Controls from CIS, the HITRUST Common Security Framework, GDPR which protects the security and privacy of EU citizens' personal information and COSO which is a joint initiative of five professional organizations.

CYBERSECURITY FRAMEWORKS OF TOMORROW

There are governance changes coming very soon that will change the face of cybersecurity and the cybersecurity workforce of tomorrow indefinitely. Those changes originate from the fact that government organizations are simply through with dealing with vendors, partners, employees, and contractors that do not apply the same level of cybersecurity awareness and practices that they implement. So much so that a new framework has been created and implemented that will require anyone working under contract with the US government to demonstrate their ability to secure their data and communications and even their workforce before engaging in any business or operational activities with the government. This framework is the Cybersecurity Maturity Model Certification or the CMMC.

Cybersecurity Maturity Model Certification

The CMMC is a system of compliance levels that helps the government, specifically the Department of Defense (DoD), determine whether an organization has the security necessary to work with controlled or otherwise vulnerable data. Companies that are interested in working with the DoD will need to be CMMC-rated and follow specific CMMC regulations.

Generally, this is done by building and following a CMMC framework and using CMMC best practices.

In 2021, DoD announced the strategic direction of the CMMC program, marking the completion of an internal program assessment led by senior leaders across the Department. The enhanced "CMMC 2.0" program maintains the program's original goal of safeguarding sensitive information, while simplifying the CMMC standard and providing additional clarity on cybersecurity regulatory, policy, and contracting requirements, focusing the most advanced cybersecurity standards and third-party assessment requirements on companies supporting the highest priority programs, and increasing department oversight of professional and ethical standards in the assessment ecosystem (Fig. 5).

The DoD states that together, these enhancements ensure accountability for companies to implement cybersecurity standards while minimizing barriers in compliance with DoD requirements, instill a collaborative culture of cybersecurity

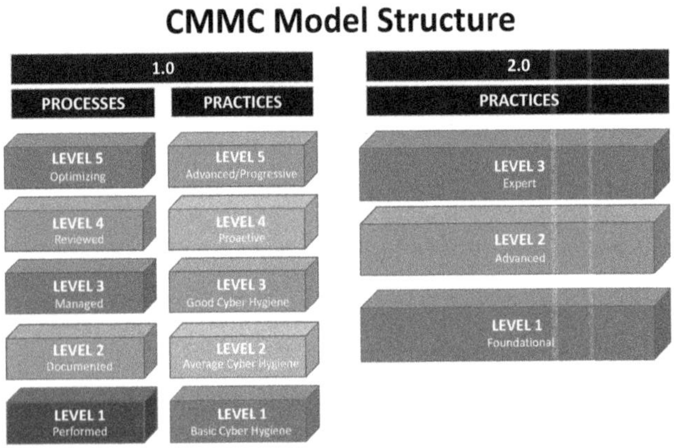

CMMC Model Structure

Source: Based on https://www.acq.osd.mil/cmmc/model.html.

Fig. 5. Cybersecurity Maturity Model.

and cyber resilience, and enhance public trust in the CMMC ecosystem, while increasing overall ease of execution.

The Solarium Report

The cybersecurity workforce of the future will need to deeper embrace the traditional values of law enforcement and the apprehension and prosecution of cyber criminals. To that extent, the deterrence of cyber threats in a perimeter security model will no longer be acceptable as more focus is now being placed on the efficient identification of cyber criminals and their criminal acts. The first movements toward consolidated efforts to achieve that can be found in the Solarium Commission's report of 2020.

In 2020, the Cyberspace Solarium Commission advocated a new strategic approach to cybersecurity using layered cyber deterrence. The desired end state of layered cyber deterrence is a reduced probability and impact of cyberattacks of significant consequence (Cyberspace solarium commission report, 2020). The strategy outlines three ways to achieve this including shaping behavior by advocating that the United States must work with allies and partners to promote responsible behavior in cyberspace, denying benefits by advocating that the United States must deny benefits to adversaries who have long exploited cyberspace to their advantage, and by imposing costs by advocating that the United States must maintain the capability, capacity, and credibility needed to retaliate against actors who target America in and through cyberspace.

The commission's findings include five propositions that are potential national, and even global, driving forces toward the next big cybersecurity initiative and framework. The following propositions are discussed in detail in the report; however, Table 5 summarizes these ideas.

Table 5. Cyberspace Solarium Commission Report Proposals.

Cyberspace Solarium Commission Report Proposals

1	Deterrence is possible in cyberspace	Today most cyber actors feel undeterred, if not emboldened, to target our personal data and public infrastructure. In other words, through our inability or unwillingness to identify and punish our cyber adversaries, we are signaling that interfering in American elections or stealing billions in US intellectual property is acceptable. The federal government and the private sector must defend themselves and strike back with speed and agility.
2	Deterrence relies on a resilient economy.	During the Cold War, our best minds were tasked with developing continuity of Government plans to ensure that the government could survive and the nation could recover after a nuclear strike. We need similar planning today to ensure that we can reconstitute in the aftermath of a national-level cyberattack. We also need to ensure that our economy continues to run. We recommend that the government institutes a continuity of the Economy plan to ensure that we can rapidly restore critical functions across corporations and industry sectors, and get the economy back up and running after a catastrophic cyberattack. Such a plan is a fundamental pillar of deterrence, a way to tell our adversaries that we, as a society, will survive to defeat them with speed and agility if they launch a major cyberattack against us.
3	Deterrence requires	We need to elevate and empower existing cyber agencies, particularly the Cybersecurity and Infrastructure Security Agency (CISA), and

Table 5. (*Continued*)

Cyberspace Solarium Commission Report Proposals

government reform.	create new focal points for coordinating cybersecurity in the executive branch and Congress. To that end, we recommend the creation of a National Cyber Director with oversight from new congressional Cybersecurity committees, but our goal is not to create more bureaucracy with new and duplicative roles and organizations. Rather, we propose giving existing organizations the tools they need to act with speed and agility to defend our networks and impose costs on our adversaries. The key is CISA, which we have tried to empower as the lead agency for federal cybersecurity and the private sector's preferred partner. We want working at CISA to become so appealing to young professionals interested in national service that it competes with the National Security Agency (NSA), the Federal Bureau of Investigation (FBI), Google, and Facebook for top-level talent and wins.
4 Deterrence will require private-sector entities to step up and strengthen their security posture.	Most of our critical infrastructure is owned by the private sector. That is why we make certain recommendations, such as establishing a cloud security certification or modernizing corporate accountability reporting requirements. We do not want to saddle the private sector with onerous and counterproductive regulations, nor do we want to force companies to hand over their data to the federal government. We are not the Chinese Communist Party, and indeed our best path to beating our adversaries is to stay free and innovative. But we need C-suite executives to take cyber seriously since they are on the front lines. With support from the federal government, private-sector entities must

Table 5. (*Continued*)

Cyberspace Solarium Commission Report Proposals

		be able to act with speed and agility to stop cyberattackers from breaking out in their networks and the larger array of networks on which the nation relies.
5	Election security must become a priority.	The American people still do not have the assurance that our election systems are secure from foreign manipulation. If we don't get election security right, deterrence will fail and future generations will look back with longing and regret on the once-powerful American Republic and wonder how we screwed the whole thing up. We believe we need to continue appropriations to fund election infrastructure modernization at the state and local levels. At the same time, states and localities need to pay their fair share to secure elections, and they can draw on useful resources, such as nonprofits, that can act with greater speed and agility across all 50 states to secure elections from the bottom up rather than waiting for top-down direction and funding. We also need to ensure that regardless of the method of casting a vote, paper or electronic, a paper audit trail exists.

Source: https://www.solarium.gov/report.

EXPERT OPINION

Matthew Pascucci, Security Engineer

In the foreseeable future, most companies and organizations will not require their cybersecurity employees to be highly skilled in AI and ML technologies and techniques but there will be an increasing need and expectancy of cybersecurity employees to be well versed and skilled in data analytics and data manipulation. The primary purpose for this would be to collect data from varied sources, aggregate that data, and manipulate that data to create some sort of picture of what may have happened during an attempted breach and what the MO of a suspected cyberattacker may have been. Without those skill sets there is simply too much data from too many discrete and individual sources on a computer network for any human to sort through manually and try to come up with some sort of analysis. That being said, there will be some companies and organizations that use AI and ML technologies as an inherent part of their daily operations and to be part of the security team for those organizations; it will be an absolute necessity to be highly functional in these areas. Either way, AI and ML technologies and approaches are here to stay and will become an integral part of the cybersecurity industry as both cybercriminals and cyber professionals both use the technologies to gain competitive advantages against each other. The requirement for the cyber worker to have those skills will simply be determined by how and if the organization is employing those solutions into their regular operations.

The cybersecurity workforce of the future and the organizations that drive it will be expecting more from their cybersecurity recruits and security teams as more technology becomes available to them to combat more complex and advanced cyber threats and threat actors. These organizations will approach this in several ways. One way will be to implement their vendors and security solutions providers as an extension of their organizations which will allow their own employees to focus on their specialties. A second approach will be to hire dedicated cybersecurity employees in-house which will give them access to the data they need to create truly secure solutions, and a third approach will be a hybrid solution where the security vendor does much of the security analysis while dedicated cybersecurity employees focus on using corporate network data from vendor and in-house solutions to identify vulnerabilities on the network that need to be addressed. In any situation the future of the cybersecurity workforce will vary on the strategy that the organization decides to put in place based on their needs.

With the rapid addition of a multitude of wireless devices joining IoT, the securing of IoT segments of networks will become more standardized as the technology becomes more and more prevalent and expected. The current challenges with weak security on IoT technologies should improve but will never be as powerful as security solutions running on powerful desktops and servers, and for this reason, the proper knowledge and skill sets of cybersecurity workers of the future will require them to have a solid understanding and working knowledge of how to properly secure and segment the sections of networks where IoT technologies reside. That may not pertain to every cybersecurity employee but every cybersecurity worker will need to have a strong understanding of the workings of IoT solutions so that they can add and configure them efficiently and effectively without introducing a new vulnerability to the organization's network infrastructure.

CASE-BASED SCENARIO

In June 2015, the United States Office of Personnel Management (OPM) discovered that the background investigation records of current, former, and prospective federal employees and contractors had been stolen. OPM and the interagency incident response team had concluded with high confidence that sensitive information, including the Social Security Numbers (SSNs) of 21.5 million individuals, was stolen from the background investigation databases. This included 19.7 million individuals that applied for a background investigation and 1.8 million nonapplicants, primarily spouses or cohabitants of applicants. Some records also include findings from interviews conducted by background investigators and approximately 5.6 million include fingerprints. Usernames and passwords that background investigation applicants used to fill out their forms were also stolen.

To place this breach into some sort of context, the recovery costs from this breach would have included employee time and consultant time to bring all systems back up online, mitigate the threat from happening again, and in identifying the ultimate cause of the breach. Additionally, the costs of addressing the loss of personal data from a legal and financial perspective would have also been astronomical, and the unknown losses from identity theft of individuals whose information was stolen is almost impossible to calculate but could be in the tens of millions of dollars.

Now for a thought experiment for you to discuss with your colleagues and peers. Why did the breach happen? Was a governance framework used to implement their security controls? Were there policies in place and enforced? Was there qualified staff in place before and during the breach that were even capable of identifying a threat and also of mitigating it before it became a risk to the organization's data? Was a vendor allowed to conduct business using department data that was not using a governance framework to secure their data? What was the risk appetite of the department? What would the cost be to make sure all of this was in place versus the aggregate loss and cost of a single cybersecurity breach? What happens if it happens again tomorrow?

2

THE CURRENT AND FUTURE TECHNOLOGY OF CYBERSECURITY

The cybersecurity workforce of tomorrow will need to utilize and embrace the current technologies that are securing our networks and sensitive data, but also understand new merging technologies that are each finding their place in the cyber domain as useful and strategically important in combating clear and present dangers to information security. In this chapter, we discuss the various technologies that are in use today for general information technology purposes, the specific technologies being used for cybersecurity purposes, and finally, new and emerging technologies that will undoubtedly play a role in future cybersecurity deterrents and are representative of new skill sets that the cybersecurity workforce of tomorrow will need to embrace and gain experience in to be successful.

CURRENT TECHNOLOGIES

Information Systems

There are several definitions of information systems that include "The study of complementary networks of hardware and software that people and organizations use to collect, filter, process, create, and distribute data," "Combinations of hardware, software, and telecommunications networks that people build and use to collect, create, and distribute useful data, typically in organizational settings," and "Interrelated components working together to collect, process, store, and disseminate information to support decision making, coordination, control, analysis, and visualization in an organization" (Bourgeois, Smith, Wang, & Mortati, 2019).

Computer Hardware

An information system is made up of six components including hardware, software, data, people, processes, and telecommunications. The physical parts of computing devices, those that you can actually touch, are referred to as hardware. Computer hardware encompasses digital devices that you can physically touch. This includes devices such as desktop computers, laptop computers, mobile phones, tablet computers, e-readers, storage devices, such as flash drives, input devices, such as keyboards, mice, and scanners output devices such as printers and speakers. Besides these more traditional computer hardware devices, many items that were once not considered digital devices are now becoming computerized themselves.

Computer Software

Software can be broadly divided into two categories: operating systems and application software. Operating systems manage the hardware and create the interface between the hardware and the user. Application software is the category of programs that do something useful for the user. Operating systems provide several essential functions, including managing the hardware resources of the computer, providing the user-interface components, and providing a platform for software developers to write applications. All computing devices run an operating system. For personal computers, the most popular operating systems are Microsoft's Windows, Apple's OS X, and different versions of Linux. Smartphones and tablets run operating systems as well, such as Apple's iOS, Google's Android and Microsoft's Windows Mobile. The second major category of software is application software. Application software is, essentially, software that allows the user to accomplish some goal or purpose like Microsoft Word or iTunes as general examples.

Computer Networking

Computer networking really began in the 1960s with the birth of the internet; however, while the internet and web were evolving, corporate networking was also taking shape in the form of local area networks and client-server computing. Computer networking refers to connected computing devices such as laptops, desktops, servers, smartphones, and tablets and an array of Internet of Things (IoT) devices such as cameras, door locks, doorbells, refrigerators, audiovisual systems, thermostats, and sensors that communicate with one another. A sample computer network can be seen in Fig. 6.

Specialized devices such as switches, routers, and access points form the foundation of computer networks. In the 1990s, when the internet came of age, internet technologies began to pervade all areas of the organization. More common methods of internet access in today are through Wi-Fi. Wi-Fi is a technology that takes an internet signal and converts it into radio waves. These radio waves can be picked up within a

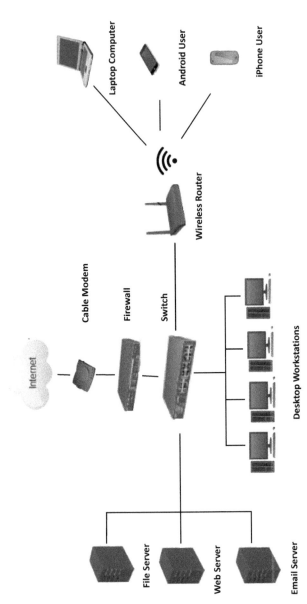

Source: Based on https://www.mydraw.com/diagrams-network-diagram-index.

Fig. 6. Sample Computer Network.

radius of approximately 65 feet by devices with a wireless adapter. Several Wi-Fi specifications have been developed over the years, starting with 802.11b (1999), followed by the 802.11g specification in 2003, and 802.11n in 2009. Each new specification improved the speed and range of Wi-Fi, allowing for more uses. One of the primary places where Wi-Fi is being used is in the home. Home users are purchasing Wi-Fi routers, connecting them to their broadband connections, and then connecting multiple devices via Wi-Fi.

Computer and Network Security

Network security is a broad term that covers a multitude of technologies, devices, and processes. In its simplest term, it is a set of rules and configurations designed to protect the integrity, confidentiality, and accessibility of computer networks and data using both software and hardware technologies. Every organization, regardless of size, industry, or infrastructure requires a degree of network security solutions in place to protect it from the ever-growing landscape of cyber threats in the wild today.

Hardware and Software Security Solutions

The security of all hardware and software components used in electronic devices is called computer security. Individual computers and those systems that broadcast messages communicate with each other globally and comprise billions of pages of graphics, texts, and other sources of information through the internet. The purpose of computer security includes the protection of data and property from corruption, theft, or natural disaster while allowing the data and property to stay accessible and productive to its intended customers. Hardware security is a form of security that secures machine and peripheral hardware from threats while software security is a form of security that secures software from threats and risks.

The Cybersecurity Toolbox

Cybersecurity software and tools are a must for any person operating as a cybersecurity professional today and are used to perform and assure functions and efficacy in the areas of application security, information security, network security, disaster recovery, and operational security. It needs to be maintained for various types of cyber threats like ransomware, malware, social engineering, and phishing. Cybersecurity software and tools can be categorized into different types including network security monitoring tools, encryption tools, web vulnerability scanning tools, network defense wireless tools, packet sniffers, antivirus software, firewall public key infrastructure (PKI) services, managed detection services, and penetration testing.

EMERGING TECHNOLOGIES IN CYBERSECURITY

Artificial Intelligence and Machine Learning

The cybersecurity workforce of tomorrow will be faced with an evolving inclusion of machine learning (ML) capabilities into most cybersecurity software and hardware solutions but also into the development of more robust and complex attacks by the cybercriminals. Attacks are getting more and more sophisticated and new types of attacks are being introduced every day. Our current security systems work well when it comes to known attacks, but new types of attacks make them obsolete sometimes. Segments of the cybersecurity workforce of tomorrow will need to use ML software available from companies like Apache and Amazon. A comprehensive grouping of ML software solutions can be found in Fig. 7.

Artificial Intelligence (AI) systems if fed with enough data can work well at predicting such attacks so that we can stop them. Especially with the rise of Deep Learning (DL), this has become much easier as they are good when it comes to dealing with huge amounts of data (Chaudhary, Detroja, Prajapati, & Sha, 2020). The main advantage of AI-based systems is that they work even when the attacks have never been seen before. It fits a high dimensional curve that separates normal and malicious traffic. Therefore, if it detects unusual activity, which is different from normal, then it generates an alarm.

AI is the comprehensive scientific system with varying branches in math, computer science, and philosophy that aims to develop another intelligent system that shows intelligence properties. ML is an essential factor in modern research and business. ML algorithms automatically build a mathematical

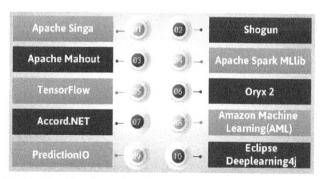

Fig. 7. Machine Learning Software Options.

model by using sample data which is called training data to make decisions without being specifically arranged (Tao, Akhtar, & Jiayuan, 2021).

The future of cybersecurity will pit AI against AI. It is expected that the scale, scope, and frequency of cyberattacks will increase disruptively with attackers harnessing AI to develop attacks that are even more targeted, sophisticated, and evasive. At the same time, analysts in security operation centers are being increasingly overwhelmed in their efforts to keep up with the tasks of detecting, managing, and responding to attacks (Chaudhary et al., 2020). Since cybercrimes are becoming increasingly complex, cyber security approaches are needed to be more robust and intelligent. This will allow defense mechanisms to make real-time decisions that can react effectively to sophisticated attacks – the use of AI in particular in the fight against cybercrimes. In a review of AI methods in defense against cybercrime, it was found that artificial smart methods contribute remarkably to cybercrimes by significantly improving intrusion detection systems (IDS) and that computer complexity, model training times, and false alarms have been reduced (Tao et al., 2021).

Intrusion Detection Systems

In the future it will be more important than ever to have your system identify anomalies on your network and to know, before you do, there is something wrong. With the steady growth of up to 20 billion connected devices on the internet now, the ability to identify who is contacting your network and for what reason is far past any human or even machine capabilities. We need systems that think and evaluate a variety of attributes based on what that system knows to be normal and acceptable behaviors and what constitutes an anomaly or something that should not be happening. The cybersecurity workforce of tomorrow needs to understand the role of AI and ML in the protection of sensitive data.

A network security system requires antivirus, firewalls, and IDS. IDS help us determine unauthorized system behavior. There are two types of intrusions including internal intrusion and external intrusion. Network analysis for IDS comprises three types of analysis usually including misuse-based, anomaly-based, and hybrid. The future of AI and intrusion detection relies on researchers who are focusing on how we can use technologies like ML and DL to create IDSs. Some more famous ML algorithms include K Nearest Neighbor (KNN), Support Vector Machines (SVM), Decision Tree, and Bayes. Deep Boltzmann Machines (DBM), Convolutional Neural Network (CNN), and Long Short Term Memory (LSTM) are examples of Deep Learning (DL) algorithms (Chaudhary et al., 2020).

To cope, the security industry and practitioners are experimenting with the application of AI and ML technologies in different areas of security operations. These include a diverse set of areas such as detecting behaviors and malware, extracting and consolidating threat intelligence, reasoning over security alerts, and recommending countermeasures and/ or protective measures. At the same time, adversarial attacks on ML systems have become an indisputable threat. Attackers can compromise the training of ML models by injecting malicious data into the training set creating poisoning attacks, or by crafting adversarial samples that exploit the blind spots of ML models at test time creating evasion attacks.

A significant advantage of AI systems in cybersecurity is that they will free up a huge amount of time for IT employees. AI is most commonly used to detect threats and attacks. The systems are developed in such a way that it must be able to act quickly to the situation on its own (Geluvaraj, Satwik, & Ashok Kumar, 2019). This freedom will be important as the cybersecurity workforce of the future will be dealing with a rapid increase in international clashes in cyberspace. This may include attacks on infrastructure and utilities, as well as damaging normal operations of governments, financial bodies, and traditional society institutions such as banks, press, law enforcement, and judicial. The role of the cyber-security worker and knowledge of AI, ML, and DL in avoiding cybercrime in future will be critical.

Blockchain Technology

One technology that first originated in a white paper in 2008 (Nakamoto, 2008) and is primarily known for its use in cryptocurrencies is blockchain. Blockchain is an important technology for the future of cybersecurity based on its level of security due to its powerful encryption methods and its generally accepted immutability, and continued research and commercialization may ultimately lead to the technology being widely used in other databases and file storage struc-tures outside of cryptocurrencies. Blockchain technology has recently been used for cybersecurity due to the robustness and integrity-preserving nature of its design. Blockchain technol-ogies applied to IoV can improve various attributes of IoV including security, privacy, reputation, distributed, decen-tralized, data sharing, authentication, and trust-based approaches (Kumar et al., 2021). An example of the block-chain encryption process can be found in Fig. 8.

As an overview, blockchain is a distributed database or ledger that is shared among the nodes of a computer network. As a database, a blockchain stores information electronically in digital format. The innovation with a blockchain is that it guarantees the fidelity and security of a record of data and generates trust without the need for a trusted third party. One

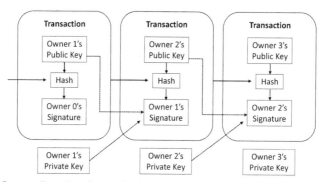

Source: Based on Comparitech.com - https://www.comparitech.com/crypto/cryptography-blockchain/.

Fig. 8. Blockchain Encryption Process.

key difference between a typical database and a blockchain is how the data are structured. A blockchain collects information together in groups, known as blocks, that hold sets of information. Blocks have certain storage capacities and, when filled, are closed and linked to the previously filled block, forming a chain of data known as the blockchain (Hayes, 2023). All new information that follows that freshly added block is compiled into a newly formed block that will then also be added to the chain once filled. This data structure inherently makes an irreversible timeline of data when implemented in a decentralized nature. When a block is filled, it is set in stone and becomes a part of this timeline. Each block in the chain is given an exact timestamp when it is added to the chain.

Quantum Computing

The cybersecurity workforce of tomorrow will need to embrace changes in encryption and cryptography advances.

The only real way to protect data once it leaves the organization's protective environment is to scramble the data so badly and in such a complex way that nobody, even a machine, can unscramble. We see this in modern encryption methods like Rivest-Shamir-Adelman (RSA) that use Advanced Encryption Standards (AES) to protect the data before it leaves the sender's computer. However, this encryption is only difficult to break because of the processors we are using that can process a 0 or a 1 at one single time. If it were possible to bypass this limitation, then the modern encryption would fail. This is the current concern with quantum processors that eliminate the need for static 0s and 1s and rely on quantum entanglement and superpositioning to create processors that can process potentially unlimited bits, called qubits in quantum, at one time. This is leading to a new concept called quantum resistant encryption and is a concern for the workforce of tomorrow. A quantum processor is not much larger than a traditional processor used in your home desktop computer but the supporting machinery to make the processor function is quite considerable.

Quantum computing is a rapidly emerging technology that harnesses the laws of quantum mechanics to solve problems too complex for classical computers. These machines are very different from the classical computers. For some problems, even supercomputers are not powerful enough to solve the problems given to them. Supercomputers are very large classical computers, often with thousands of CPU and GPU cores. However, even supercomputers struggle to solve certain kinds of problems when asked to solve a problem with a high degree of complexity ("What is quantum computing?", 2021).

Complex problems are problems with lots of variables interacting in complicated ways. A supercomputer might be great at difficult tasks like sorting through a big database of weather anomalies but it may struggle to see the subtle patterns in that data that determine how those various parts of the jetstream behave in relation to weather events happening thousands of miles away. Quantum algorithms take a new approach to these sorts of complex problems by creating multidimensional spaces where the patterns linking individual data points emerge. Classical computers cannot create these computational spaces, so they cannot find patterns or relationships, for example, in the weather anomalies above. As quantum hardware scales and new algorithms advance, they could tackle things like weather anomalies and patterns that are too complex for any supercomputer.

Instead of bits or traditional zeros and ones, quantum computers use Josephson junctions as superconducting qubits. By firing microwave photons at these qubits, behavior can be controlled and can get them to hold, change, and read out individual units of quantum information which represents a combination of all possible configurations of the qubit and not just a zero or a one at one given time. When groups of qubits are combined in what's known as a superposition, scientists and developers can create complex, multidimensional computational spaces, and complex problems can be represented in new ways inside these spaces.

The impact of quantum computing on the cybersecurity workforce of tomorrow is considerable as the traditional approaches of threat identification and mitigation may become obsolete. The concept of nearly limitless processing power at the fingertips of future cyber criminals combined with a workforce that, potentially, has not prepared adequately for the new technology would be catastrophic and cyberattacks may quite possibly become indefensible. Although the availability of quantum computing is currently limited to a few companies like IBM and Google who make their prototype systems available to the scientific community, the presence of quantum processors in everyday life is quite a few years away.

Nevertheless, we see proactive responses by governments already in preparation for the inevitable availability of these quantum processors with the presence of things like post-quantum cryptography algorithms ("Post quantum cryptography algorithms", 2022). The cybersecurity workforce of tomorrow will not only need to understand the workings of this new technology but also as the technology evolves and requires things like new operating systems, new programming languages, and new quantum data structures, it will be imperative to make sure that the cybersecurity workforce is capable of applying and manipulating these technologies against adversaries that may be using them for malicious purposes.

The 5G Spectrum

The cybersecurity workforce of tomorrow needs to embrace the newly implemented 5G spectrum and the massive amount of data that can travel across these networks at mind-blowing speeds never seen before. The possibility of cybercriminals downloading massive amounts of data before any mitigation efforts can even be attempted is now a reality. The fifth-generation wireless networking technology popularly known as "5G" delivers ultrafast download rates, ultralow latency, massive capacity, and vastly improved user experiences (Waters, 2020). 5G finally makes it practical to connect machines, objects, and devices with fiber-like speeds over the air. 5G offers a broader range of wireless services than previous generations delivered to the end user across multiple access platforms and multilayer networks. Table 6 contains specific performance details of 5G.

Table 6. Performance Attributes of 5G.

5G Performance Details

1	Speed	5G is enough, for example, to allow a user to download a full-length feature movie to phone in seconds. 3G: 3 Mbps downloads 4G: 100 Mbps downloads 5G: 10 Gbps downloads – 10 times faster than 4G
2	Latency	5G reduces response time significantly. By cutting "lag," 5G not only heralds a veritable revolution in online gaming but also becomes essential to the success of self-driving cars and remotely operated medical devices.
3	The technology	A 5G mobile network comprises two essential components: the Radio Access Network (RAN) and the Core Network (the Core).

Source: Original table and content creation from research.

The 5G Core Network is the mobile exchange and data network that manages the mobile voice, data, and internet connections. Where previous generations (3G and 4G) focused primarily on delivering services and information to mobile phones, the 5G Core is all about integrating with the internet and cloud-based services, and it includes distributed servers across the network, further reducing latency. The Core is where key features of 5G will be managed, things like network function virtualization and network slicing for different applications and services.

It is clear that those technologies will radically change how people work, communicate, think, and even fight in the near future. They simultaneously generate great concern that state-sponsored actors could interfere and disrupt their features and services, posing a massive threat to strategically vital networks (Kanellos, 2021). 5G technology has the potential to drastically increase the attack surface and the number of entry points for hackers because of the large number of connected devices including things like baby monitors to refrigerators with weaker security features. However, not only do low-cost interconnected devices introduce vulnerabilities, the communication between these devices can be the weakest link in 5G's security. Similarly, cloud computing technology consists of computer storage, front-end technology like laptops, desktops, and networking infrastructure, and cloud-based applications which may also be disrupted and exploited. This risk applies both to the commercial clouds as well as the smaller-scale cloud services used for classified operations and secured sensitive data.

Although the cybersecurity workforce of the future may not be directly involved in the building out and enhancement of the 5G network as that will mostly be electrical engineers and telecommunications experts, the future cybersecurity worker will need to be able to create tools and automate processes to handle the enormous amount of data that will be moving through these larger communication pipes which will be in stark contrast to the amount of data currently moving through the existing infrastructure.

Zero-Trust Networks

The cybersecurity workforce of tomorrow will be fully embedded in cloud-based and centrally hosted and managed data on shared servers. While not so long ago, the concept of housing your sensitive data on a server owned and managed by someone else who has no direct connection to your organization would have been seen as absolute heresy, it is now almost unthinkable to buy your own servers, hire a full-time staff to manage them, and still maintain a high level of risk of data loss due to human error. For this reason, cybersecurity professionals will need to be well versed in zero-trust philosophies and architectures. Zero-trust networks increase the need for trust in data. Smarter software requires safer and more secure infrastructure (Stempfley, 2019a, 2019b). Zero Trust is a strategic approach to cybersecurity that secures an organization by eliminating implicit trust and continuously validating every stage of a digital interaction ("What is a Zero Trust Architecture", 2021). Zero-trust is designed to protect modern environments and enable digital transformation by using strong authentication methods, leveraging network segmentation, preventing lateral movement, providing Layer seven threat prevention, and simplifying granular, "least access" policies. A zero-trust architecture can be seen in Fig. 9 (Kerman, Borchert, & Rose, 2020).

Zero Trust was created based on the realization that traditional security models operate on the outdated

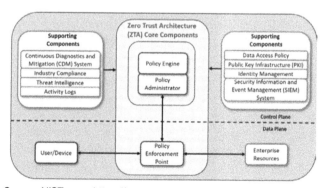

Source: NIST.gov - https://www.nccoe.nist.gov/sites/default/files/legacy-files/zt-arch-project-description-draft.pdf.

Fig. 9. Sample Zero-Trust Architecture.

assumption that everything inside an organization's network should be implicitly trusted. This implicit trust means that once on the network, users, including threat actors and malicious insiders, are free to move laterally and access or exfiltrate sensitive data due to a lack of granular security controls. The cybersecurity workforce of the future will need to be fully articulated into the zero-trust domain and be able to balance between traditional networks with hardware solutions physically inside their buildings, a cloud model where their information is stored on remotely hosted servers and the zero-trust domain where the traditional VPN is replaced with various technologies that provide the ultimate security on a cloud-based system by providing access to only those devices and users with centrally managed authorization.

Operational Technology

Operation technology (OT) is important to understand regarding the future of cybersecurity because it is used to control our operations systems including industrial control systems (ICS), building management systems, fire control systems, and physical access control mechanisms. OT is the hardware and software components of control systems used within critical infrastructures such as energy and transportation (Murray, Johnstone, & Valli, 2017). These are programmable systems or devices that interact with the physical environment or manage devices that interact with the physical environment. These systems and devices can detect or cause a direct change through the monitoring or control of devices, processes, and events. Any breach or compromise of these systems may provide access to the threat actor to damage the system, shut the system down completely, or make the system behave in a manner that would cause others physical harm or damage infrastructure causing property damage. An example might be a threat actor that compromises the OT system that controls a railroad crossing and changes the behaviors of that operation technology that puts both pedestrians and vehicles at risk.

Internet of Things

One of the most concerning areas for the future of cybersecurity and its workforce is the area of IoT. IoT describes the network of physical objects that are embedded with sensors, software, and other technologies for the purpose of connecting and exchanging data with other devices and systems over the internet. These devices range from ordinary household objects to sophisticated industrial tools. With more than 7 billion connected IoT devices today, experts are expecting this number to grow to 10 billion by 2020 and 22 billion by 2025 ("What is IOT", 2022). As the goal in cybersecurity is to become operationally resilient, which means in part that employees of an organization are trained to prevent and handle a cybersecurity incident, it is a growing public concern that more threats and vulnerabilities with IOT devices and systems are being discovered and exploited by adversaries each day. In particular, ICS are at a higher risk because their components were not designed with cybersecurity in mind (Hott, Zohner, Fetzer, & Malzahn, 2019). This being true, the most worrisome of the modern cyberattacks that may contribute to the most chaotic outcomes would be the IOT attack that could render, for example, thousands of medical devices and even implants to work improperly or not at all. With increased risk to ICS, It is vital that the employees who work on the system are trained in best practices and the latest threats of cybersecurity. Research has shown that there are currently no curriculum standards for an ICS cybersecurity professional, which may contribute to the issues faced during the hiring process. In fact, most individuals require extensive post-hire training before they can begin normal operations (Hott & Zohner, 2019). The world of IOT does not involve or include complex and mature devices and equipment like desktop computers, smart phones, or even tablets but more embedded systems and chipsets that are programmed at the factory and then controlled by a publicly available app that anyone can download usually for free.

With us rapidly approaching 22 billion access points on the internet, the cybersecurity workforce of tomorrow will not able to dismiss these devices as entities that are out of their realm of interest because they are not connected as a user device with associated operating systems and user-focused interfaces, and they will need to understand and embrace the IOT devices included the control board limitations and weaknesses of various devices, firmware vulnerabilities, and most of all how these device are being connected to the TCB or trusted computer base.

Vehicle Security

The cybersecurity workforce of tomorrow will emerge in a network of vehicles that enables any vehicle on the internet to become a node with potential access to its onboard computer that controls its steering, braking, cruise control, environmental systems, and lighting. This makes every vehicle a potential target for any cyberattacker in the world. The IoV is a network that interconnects pedestrians, cars, and parts of urban infrastructure. It uses various sensors, software, in-built hardware, and types of connection to enable reliable and continuous communication. IoV strives to make transportation more autonomous, safe, fast, and efficient, reducing resource waste and detrimental impacts on the environment ("What is the Internet of Vehicles (IoV)", 2022).

Recently, the IoV concept is becoming very popular due to sharing of the data between vehicles and the infrastructure. The sharing of data is very important for enhancing vehicular services, but at the same time makes IoV vulnerable to security and privacy issues. IoV is very vulnerable to malicious attacks due to its self-organizing nature and the open source nature of its implementations. This exposes the smart and interconnected vehicles to a variety of privacy and security threats, such as a remote hijacking or location tracking of vehicles. Thus, the security for IoV environment is critical (Kumar et al., 2021).

Today, cybersecurity affects each one of us on a multitude of levels. Our professional work, our personal lives, and even our vehicles depend on connectivity and technology that runs on complex software. Applied to vehicles, cybersecurity takes on an even more important role in that systems and components that govern safety must be protected from harmful attacks, unauthorized access, damage, or anything else that might interfere with safety functions. As an example of the risks of vehicle security, two researchers were able to breach a Jeep Cherokee being used for the study and take charge of the vehicle's controls using a laptop from a house miles away. As part of the experiment, the team cut the Jeep's brakes, causing the vehicle to slide into a ditch (Allison, 2016). In addition to manipulating the Jeep's controls remotely, the research team was able to track targeted GPS coordinates, measure speed, and trace routes.

Chaos Engineering

The cybersecurity workforce of tomorrow will be tasked with maintaining system stability and uptimes for global networks and corporate systems that may lose millions of dollars per second if subjected to a malicious cybersecurity attack. It will be imperative, in some organizations and positions, to have experience and training in testing network vulnerabilities and weaknesses through a process called penetration testing or pentesting. One method on the cutting edge of penetration testing is known as chaos engineering and will most likely play an important role in the future of cybersecurity and its workforce. Chaos engineering was originated by Netflix in 2008 and was based on various components of chaos theory. It is the discipline of experimenting on a system in order to build confidence in the system's capability to withstand turbulent conditions in production. As systems become more complex, cloud-based, and more distributed, it is changing the game for software engineers and the cybersecurity workforce of tomorrow. Tools like Chaos Monkey, a tool created and provided by Netflix to launch attack code against an infrastructure, allow us to apply chaos engineering principles to things like cybersecurity. A sample workflow from Chaos Monkey can be seen in Fig. 10.

In chaos theory, random or unpredictable behavior is studied in systems governed by deterministic laws. By using tools like Chaos Monkey on a computer network specifically focusing on attack routines, the effects that the system experiences can be observed which would never have been able to have been predicted using standard or individual testing procedures. This allows cybersecurity teams to prepare better for a single or even a series of linked and interrelated cyberattacks that may occur in the future. The cybersecurity workforce of the future will be exposed to this emerging process as an increasingly useful tool and will be combined

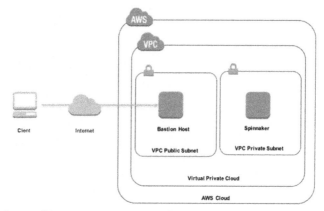

Source: Chaos.gremlin.com - https://chaos.gremlin.com/rs/251-JGH-155/images/2018-06-Chaos_Monkey_Microsite_PDF.pdf.

Fig. 10. Sample Chaos Monkey Workflow.

with the normal procedures of today like penetration testing or vulnerability analysis. The future cybersecurity professional will need to use the blanketing theories of chaos engineering combined with the applicable business processes of patching, penetration testing, packet analysis, and so forth to identify potential weaknesses in their systems so they can apply the proper solutions to the identified problems.

KEITH STRASSBERG, CHIEF OPERATING OFFICER, CYBERSAFE SOLUTIONS, LLP

The cybersecurity workforce of tomorrow will need to evolve with the advances in technology that are evolving. With regards to the use of AI and ML as part of the daily activities of a future cybersecurity worker, it will depend on the organization they are working for. As an example, if the organization is creating original and unique software solutions to autonomously identify anomalies on the network using a very innovative and proprietary technique, then yes the cybersecurity worker would need to be well versed in AI and ML data analysis and programming techniques. However, if the organization has decided to adopt a "blackbox" and vendor-driven approach to their cybersecurity, then the organizational worker may simply need a general understanding of how AI and ML technologies are affecting their network while the more technology-driven work is happening at the vendor's site. In the future, and even now in many respects, industry will not be as tolerant of workers entering or transitioning to the workforce without demonstrable and more advanced general computing skills of which cybersecurity will be a core requirement. In the future, organizations simply will not accept workers who represent risk to their cybersecurity defenses.

Technology adoption at an organization is generally established through innovation. If an organization is innovative and realizes how that innovation, if implemented, can improve their organizations efficiency or profitability, then the technologies that drive that innovation will be adopted and the workers will need to either have or will need to learn that technology to continue to be effective employees at that organization. As an example, if an organization realizes that the use of ML algorithms on their existing network traffic data can greatly improve security then that organization may now need to consider cybersecurity workers for the future that already know how to implement AI and ML technologies. Technology solutions with weak embedded security will not be widely implemented in the future as organizations and their vendors are much more cautious, and even mandated under various frameworks, to make sure that their implemented solutions meet certain security requirements regardless of the purpose of that solution. The days of the insecure software solution implementation by the organization are over and this means that the creators and providers of these solutions will need to make sure that they have more advanced workers and engineers on staff so that they can compete against other providers.

CASE BASED SCENARIO

Professional networking giant LinkedIn saw data associated with 700 million of its users posted on a dark web forum in June 2021, impacting more than 90% of its user base. A hacker going by the moniker of "God User" used data scraping techniques by exploiting the site's application programming interface (API) before eliminating a dataset of around 500 million customers. They then followed up by bragging that they were selling the full 700 million customer database. While LinkedIn argued that as no sensitive, private personal data was exposed, the incident was a violation of its terms of service rather than a data breach, a scraped data sample posted by God User contained information including email addresses, phone numbers, geolocation records, genders, and other social media details, which would give malicious actors plenty of data to craft convincing, follow-on social engineering attacks in the wake of the leak, as warned by the UK's National Cyber Security Centre (NCSC). As a thought experiment to discuss with your colleagues and peers, consider what technologies were currently in place at LinkedIn that were breached and ask yourselves the following. Why did the technology fail? Were they configured correctly? Did they exist at all? Was this human error of some sort? Could emerging technologies like AI and ML or even blockchain have prevented the breach? Could God User have been identified by an IDS that used ML and finally, why were the data not encrypted? Could quantum resistant encryption, if available, have prevented the breach?

3

THE CYBERHERO AND THE CYBERCRIMINAL

INTRODUCTION

Cybersecurity is a very interesting field due the fact that it encompasses, in some respects, two individual fields including Information Technology and Law Enforcement. A cybersecurity professional needs to understand all of the functionality of the six-component IT framework including hardware, software, people, data, processes and telecommunications, and the security controls and analysis tools to assure secure network operations, but they also need to understand the criminal element and the methods of operation or MOs of cybercriminals so that they know what to look for during a suspected breach and how to apply the appropriate mitigation techniques. Conversely, we are seeing a considerable increase in cybercriminals and threat actors with a very high level of skills and abilities making it a very confrontational environment between the cybersecurity professionals who are dedicated to protecting the personal data and personal safety of other people and the cybercriminals who are intent on acquiring and capitalizing on people's data through nefarious, dangerous, and sometimes deadly practices. In this chapter we discuss the two opposing actors in the cybersecurity arena and we refer to them as the Cyberheroes and the Cybercriminals.

CYBERHEROES AND CYBERCRIMINALS

Cyberheroes are characterized by a combination of personal attributes that include an ability to think critically, solve problems, and able to work at a high technical level and ability, but they also demonstrate a distinct quality of character and morality where they want to make a difference and feel responsibility for protecting potential victims of cybercrime and ultimately catching the bad guys. There are several factors and inherent traits that contribute to an individual becoming a Cyberhero.

Cyberheroes are usually very passionate about security. A passion for cybersecurity is very motivating and can come from the sense that you're making people's lives better. They are usually good, adaptive communicators and can communicate about both technical and business aspects. They are lifelong learners and have a thirst for knowledge. The security industry is one of constant change, from cybercriminals employing new methods of attack to new regulations and new tools, security professionals must be in constant learning mode. They enjoy problem-solving and challenges and feel that cybersecurity is a chess game. Cyberheroes usually have a flexible viewpoint and the ability to see the entire picture is important in cybersecurity. They are usually good planners and project managers and everything in security translates to a project. Cyberheroes have the ability to delegate and cybersecurity is a team event. The ability to delegate, share duties, and seek opinions of others is a strong attribute in the cybersecurity world. They have a vision for the future and have the ability to anticipate new and emerging threats. They enjoy engaging with people and ultimately teams of people are responsible for protecting data not just individuals. Finally, a cyberhero is usually both self-driven and self-managed and can get things done without a lot of supervision.

Cybercriminals are more difficult to identify their attributes and qualities since they are less accessible for obvious reasons. However, researchers from different disciplines have attempted to explore different dimensions of the issues surrounding cybercrime behavior and understanding the steps in the process of committing crime, and understanding the conditions that facilitate its commission, helps us to see how we can intervene to frustrate crime (Willison, 2006). Criminal profiling is the process of investigating and examining criminal behavior in order to help identify the type of person responsible (Savino & Turvey, 2011). According to (Stevens, 2011), profiling is an educated attempt to provide specific information as to the type of individual who committed a certain crime. A profile based on characteristics, patterns, or factors of uniqueness that distinguish certain individuals from the general population (Jahankhani & Al-Metrat, 2012).

Based on the concepts above, we know that cybercrime is compatible with young adults' lifestyle and familiarity and requires little knowledge. Moreover, barriers to entry related to psychological and financial costs, risks, and investments are low (Richet, 2015). Cyberspace transforms the scale and scope of offense and has its own limits, interactional forms, roles, and rules; and it has its own forms of criminal endeavor. According to Yar (2005), the novel sociointeractional features of the cyberspace environment, primarily the collapse of spatial-temporal barriers, many-to-many connectivity, and the anonymity and plasticity of online identity, make possible new forms and patterns of illicit activity. Anyone who is computer literate can become a cybercriminal (Richet, 2013).

There is still no clear definition of "cybercrime" (Fafinski, Dutton, & Margetts, 2010). In some cases, cybercrime can encompass the use of computers to assist "traditional" offending, but it can also be a crime mediated through technology (Wall, 2007) or an exclusive technological crime, such as a denial-of-service attack. Many criminal law scholars focus on the legalistic framework. For instance, Wall (2007) uses the categories of criminal law to create categories of cybercrime. Others categorize cybercrime as an offense "related to computers, related to content or against the confidentiality, integrity and availability of computer data and systems".

KNOWLEDGE, SKILLS, AND ABILITIES (KSAS)

The field of cybersecurity is a battlefield between the cybercriminals who are constantly trying to find new ways of bypassing security perimeters and accessing sensitive data to serve their own specific purposes and the cyberprofessionals or cyberheroes who are constantly trying to identify these potential and active threats to deter them before they cause costly and possible irreparable damage to their systems and information. To achieve this deterrence against the cybercriminal's efforts, the cyberprofessional has various levels of KSAs specific to the field of cybersecurity. There are various KSAs that are evident in successful cyberprofessionals and, unfortunately, also in some of the most dangerous cybercriminals that make them both very successful at their individual roles. It would be an enormous task to identify all of these roles, responsibilities, and skills for a book like this; however, we are lucky that the National Institute for Cybersecurity Education or NICE has done this for us. These KSAs are discussed in detail in the NICE Cybersecurity Framework.

THE NICE CYBERSECURITY FRAMEWORK

The Workforce Framework for Cybersecurity, commonly referred to as the NICE Framework, is a nationally focused resource to help employers develop their cybersecurity workforce. It establishes a common lexicon that describes cybersecurity work and workers regardless of where or for whom the work is performed. The NICE Framework applies across public, private, and academic sectors. The cybersecurity workforce of the future is considered in this framework which makes it a great tool for all audiences to use to grasp what is coming for them in the future.

The NICE Framework is comprised of 7 categories, A high-level grouping of common cybersecurity functions, 33 specialty areas, distinct areas of cybersecurity work, and 52 work roles which are the most detailed groupings of cybersecurity work comprised of specific KSAs required to perform tasks in a Work Role. Additionally, there are Task, Knowledge, and Skill (TKS) statements which are the core building blocks of the NICE Framework. Within the framework, a task is an activity directed toward the achievement of organizational objectives. Tasks include associated knowledge and skill statements that represent learners' potential to perform those tasks. Knowledge refers to a retrievable set of concepts within memory and skill refers to the capacity to perform an observable action. A visualization of the framework can be seen in Fig. 11.

Within the framework there are also competencies which are mechanisms for organizations to assess learners. Competencies consist of a name, description, and group of associated TKS statements. Work roles are a way of describing a grouping of work for which someone is responsible or accountable, and they are associated with groupings of tasks that constitute the work to be done.

NICE Cybersecurity Workforce Framework

- 7 Cybersecurity Workforce Categories
- 33 Specialty Areas
- 52 Cybersecurity Work Roles
- Knowledge, Skills & Abilities for Each

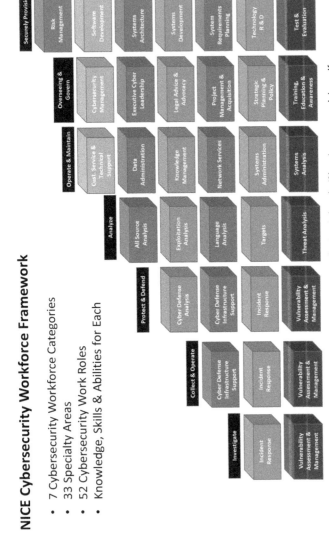

Source: Based on US DoD: https://dl.dod.cyber.mil/wp-content/uploads/cae/pdf/unclass-cae-cd_ku.pdf.

Fig. 11. NICE Cybersecurity Workforce Framework.

The cybersecurity workforce of tomorrow will comprise workers who have been identified as maintaining high levels of competency in practical applications of the KSAs. In the cybersecurity workforce of tomorrow, employers assess their cybersecurity workforce, identify critical gaps in cybersecurity staffing, and improve position descriptions and recruitment. Current and future cybersecurity workers explore work roles, KSAs, and tasks valued by employers for in-demand cybersecurity positions and academic advisors and staffing specialists support students and job seekers in designing their path toward a job in cybersecurity training and certification providers. The framework is designed to help current and future members of the cybersecurity workforce gain and demonstrate the KSAs. It is also designed for education providers as a reference to develop curriculum, courses, seminars, and research aligned to NICE framework KSAs and tasks.

The NICE Workforce Framework for Cybersecurity provides users with a common vocabulary that can be used to improve processes and practices around identifying, recruiting, developing, and retaining cybersecurity talent. It can be further applied across organizations and sectors in the development of resources and tools that define or provide guidance on workforce development, planning, training, and education. The cybersecurity workforce of tomorrow will comprise a force of unique individuals focused in specific areas of defense and deterrence and will either possess or acquire the various skill sets or KSAs identified in the next section.

CURRENT AND FUTURE CYBERSECURITY ROLES AND RESPONSIBILITIES

In today's cybersecurity workforce there are a variety of roles and responsibilities that workers fill. These rules and responsibilities are carried out at for-profit and nonprofit organizations, healthcare facilities, government, and educational facilities alike as data of all kinds have become a target for the cybercriminals as they find more and more demand for stolen data on the dark web. In this section we use the NICE cybersecurity framework to outline the various roles, responsibilities, and the definitions of these roles in the cybersecurity arena today (Table 7).

HUMAN RESOURCES AND THE CYBERSECURITY WORKFORCE OF TOMORROW

The human resources department of any organization is a sometimes grueling environment during times of staffing shortages or times like the postpandemic great resignation still plaguing HR departments for quite some time now. With regards to the cybersecurity workforce of tomorrow, there are several approaches HR departments can take to both make their department a security conscious entity and improve their security within their department, but also to attract, engage, attain, and retain quality cybersecurity employees for the long run. There is nothing more disheartening to a cybersecurity professional, a cyberhero, than to work for an organization that does not understand nor really demonstrate serious concern about the security of its organization's data. This leads to a very serious turnover issue where security employees start learning about your security and then leave quickly for other organizations and offers due to the security posture and risk appetite of your organization. There are several things HR can do to help address this, and these approaches are discussed below.

Table 7. NICE Cybersecurity Roles.

NICE Cybersecurity Work Roles

Category	Specialty Area	Work Role	Work Role Definition
Securely Provision	Risk management	Authorizing Official/ Designated Representative	Senior official or executive with the authority to formally assume responsibility for operating an information system at an acceptable level of risk to organizational operations (including mission, functions, image, or reputation), organizational assets, individuals, other organizations, and the nation (CNSSI 4009).
		Security Control Assessor	Conducts independent comprehensive assessments of the management, operational, and technical security controls and control enhancements employed within or inherited by an information technology (IT) system to determine the overall effectiveness of the controls (as defined in NIST SP 800-37).
	Software development	Software Developer	Develops, creates, maintains, and writes/codes new (or modifies existing) computer applications, software, or specialized utility programs.

Table 7. (*Continued*)

NICE Cybersecurity Work Roles

Category	Specialty Area	Work Role	Work Role Definition
		Secure Software Assessor	Analyzes the security of new or existing computer applications, software, or specialized utility programs and provides actionable results.
	Systems Architecture	Enterprise Architect	Develops and maintains business, systems, and information processes to support enterprise mission needs; develops IT rules and requirements that describe baseline and target architectures.
		Security Architect	Designs enterprise and systems security throughout the development lifecycle; translates technology and environmental conditions (e.g., law and regulation) into security designs and processes.
	Technology R&D	Research and Development Specialist	Conducts software and systems engineering and software systems research in order to develop new capabilities, ensuring cybersecurity is fully integrated. Conducts comprehensive technology research to evaluate potential vulnerabilities in cyberspace systems.

	Systems Requirements Planning	Requirements Planner	Consults with customers to evaluate functional requirements and translate functional requirements into technical solutions.
	Test and Evaluation	Testing and Evaluation Specialist	Plans, prepares, and executes tests of systems to evaluate results against specifications and requirements as well as analyze/report test results.
	Systems Development	Information Systems Security Developer	Designs, develops, tests, and evaluates information system security throughout the systems development lifecycle.
		Systems Developer	Designs, develops, tests, and evaluates information systems throughout the systems development lifecycle.
Operate and Maintain	Database Administration	Database Administrator	Administers databases and/or data management systems that allow for the storage, query, and utilization of data.
		Data Analyst	Examines data from multiple disparate sources with the goal of providing new insight. Designs and implements custom algorithms, flow processes and layouts for complex, enterprise-scale data sets used for modeling, data mining, and research purposes.
	Knowledge Management	Knowledge Manager	Responsible for the management and administration of processes and tools that enable the organization to identify, document, and access intellectual capital and information content.

Table 7. (*Continued*)

NICE Cybersecurity Work Roles

Category	Specialty Area	Work Role	Work Role Definition
	Customer Service and Technical Support	Technical Support Specialist	Provides technical support to customers who need assistance utilizing client level hardware and software in accordance with established or approved organizational process components. (i.e., Master Incident management plan, when applicable).
	Network Services	Network Operations Specialist	Plans, implements, and operates network services/systems, to include hardware and virtual environments.
	Systems Administration	System Administrator	Installs, configures, troubleshoots, and maintains hardware, software, and administers system accounts.
	Systems Analysis	Systems Security Analyst	Responsible for the analysis and development of the integration, testing, operations, and maintenance of systems security.
Oversee and Govern	Legal Advice and Advocacy	Cyber Legal Advisor	Provides legal advice and recommendations on relevant topics related to cyber law.
	Privacy Compliance	Privacy Compliance Manager	Develops and oversees privacy compliance program and privacy program staff, supporting privacy compliance needs of privacy and security executives and their teams.
	Training, Education, and Awareness	Cyber Instructional Curriculum Developer	Develops, plans, coordinates, and evaluates cyber training/ education courses, methods, and techniques based on instructional needs.

Category	Role	Description
	Cyber Instructor	Develops and conducts training or education of personnel within the cyber domain.
Cybersecurity Management	Information Systems Security Manager	Responsible for the cybersecurity of a program, organization, system, or enclave.
	COMSEC Manager	Manages the Communications Security (COMSEC) resources of an organization (CNSSI No. 4009).
Strategic Planning and Policy	Cyber Workforce Developer and Manager	Develop cyberspace workforce plans, strategies, and guidance to support cyberspace workforce manpower, personnel, training, and education requirements and to address changes to cyberspace policy, doctrine, materiel, force structure, and education and training requirements.
	Cyber Policy and Strategy Planner	Develops cyberspace plans, strategy, and policy to support and align with organizational cyberspace missions and initiatives.
Executive Cyber Leadership	Executive Cyber Leadership	Executes decision-making authorities and establishes vision and direction for an organization's cyber and cyber-related resources and/or operations.
Acquisition and Program/Project Management	Program Manager	Leads, coordinates, communicates, integrates, and is accountable for the overall success of the program, ensuring alignment with critical agency priorities.
	IT Project Manager	Directly manages information technology projects to provide a unique service or product.

Table 7. (*Continued*)

NICE Cybersecurity Work Roles

Category	Specialty Area	Work Role	Work Role Definition
		Product Support Manager	Manages the package of support functions required to field and maintain the readiness and operational capability of systems and components.
		IT Investment/Portfolio Manager	Manages a portfolio of IT capabilities that align with the overall needs of mission and business enterprise priorities.
		IT Program Auditor	Conducts evaluations of an IT program or its individual components, to determine compliance with published standards.
Protect and Defend	Cyber Defense Analysis	Cyber Defense Analyst	Uses data collected from a variety of cyber defense tools (e.g., IDS alerts, firewalls, network traffic logs) to analyze events that occur within their environments for the purposes of mitigating threats.
	Cyber Defense Infrastructure	Cyber Defense Infrastructure Support Specialist	Tests, implements, deploys, maintains, and administers the infrastructure hardware and software.
	Incident Response	Cyber Defense Incident Responder	Investigates, analyzes, and responds to cyber incidents within the network environment or enclave.

	Vulnerability Assessment and Management	Vulnerability Analyst	Performs assessments of systems and networks within the network environment or enclave and identifies where those systems/networks deviate from acceptable configurations, enclave policy, or local policy. Measures effectiveness of defense-in-depth architecture against known vulnerabilities.
Analyze	Threat Analysis	Warnings Analyst	Develops unique cyber indicators to maintain constant awareness of the status of the highly dynamic operating environment. Collects, processes, analyzes, and disseminates cyber warning assessments.
	Exploitation Analysis	Exploitation Analyst	Collaborates to identify access and collection gaps that can be satisfied through cyber collection and/or preparation activities. Leverages all authorized resources and analytic techniques to penetrate targeted networks.
	All-Source Analysis	All-Source Analyst	Analyzes data/information from one or multiple sources to conduct preparation of the environment, respond to requests for information, and submit intelligence collection and production requirements in support of planning and operations.
		Mission Assessment Specialist	Develops assessment plans and measures of performance/effectiveness. Conducts strategic and operational effectiveness assessments as required for cyber events. Determines whether systems performed as expected and provides input to the determination of operational effectiveness.

Table 7. (*Continued*)

NICE Cybersecurity Work Roles

Category	Specialty Area	Work Role	Work Role Definition
	Targets	Target Developer	Performs target system analysis, builds and/or maintains electronic target folders to include inputs from environment preparation, and/or internal or external intelligence sources. Coordinates with partner target activities and intelligence organizations, and presents candidate targets for vetting and validation.
		Target Analyst	Conducts advanced analysis of collection and open-source data to ensure target continuity; to profile targets and their activities; and develop techniques to gain more target information. Determines how targets communicate, move, operate and live based on knowledge of target technologies, digital networks, and the applications on them.
	Language Analysis	Language Analyst	Applies language and culture expertise with target/threat and technical knowledge to process, analyze, and/or disseminate intelligence information derived from language, voice and/or graphic material. Creates and maintains language-specific databases and working aids to support cyber action execution and ensure critical knowledge sharing. Provides subject matter expertise in foreign language-intensive or interdisciplinary projects.

Operate and Collect	Collection Operations	All Source-Collection Manager	Identifies collection authorities and environment; incorporates priority information requirements into collection management; develops concepts to meet leadership's intent. Determines capabilities of available collection assets, identifies new collection capabilities, and constructs and disseminates collection plans. Monitors execution of tasked collection to ensure effective execution of the collection plan.
		All Source-Collection Requirements Evaluation Manager	Evaluates collection operations and develops effects-based collection requirements strategies using available sources and methods to improve collection. Develops, processes, validates, and coordinates submission of collection requirements. Evaluates performance of collection assets and collection operations.
	Cyber Operational Planning	Cyber Intel Planner	Develops detailed intelligence plans to satisfy cyber operations requirements. Collaborates with cyber operations planners to identify, validate, and levy requirements for collection and analysis. Participates in targeting selection, validation, synchronization, and execution of cyber actions. Synchronizes intelligence activities to support organization objectives in cyberspace.

Table 7. (*Continued*)

NICE Cybersecurity Work Roles

Category	Specialty Area	Work Role	Work Role Definition
	Cyber Operations	Cyber Operations Planner	Develops detailed plans for the conduct or support of the applicable range of cyber operations through collaboration with other planners, operators, and/or analysts. Participates in targeting selection, validation, synchronization, and enables integration during the execution of cyber actions.
		Partner Integration Planner	Works to advance cooperation across organizational or national borders between cyber operations partners. Aids the integration of partner cyber teams by providing guidance, resources, and collaboration to develop best practices and facilitate organizational support for achieving objectives in integrated cyber actions.
		Cyber Operator	Conducts collection, processing, and/or geolocation of systems in order to exploit, locate, and/or track targets of interest. Performs network navigation, tactical forensic analysis, and, when directed, executing on-net operations.

Investigate	Cyber Investigation	Cyber Crime Investigator	Identifies, collects, examines, and preserves evidence using controlled and documented analytical and investigative techniques.
	Digital Forensics	Forensics Analyst	Conducts deep-dive investigations on computer-based crimes establishing documentary or physical evidence, to include digital media and logs associated with cyber intrusion incidents.
		Cyber Defense Forensics Analyst	Analyzes digital evidence and investigates computer security incidents to derive useful information in support of system/ network vulnerability mitigation.

Source: NIST: Cybersecurity Workforce Framework https://www.nist.gov/itl/applied-cybersecurity/nice/nice-framework-resource-center.

Every employee needs to practice basic cyber hygiene for a company to be safe. HR professionals handle a lot of sensitive business data. This includes employee personal information, salary details, etc., which can cause massive damage if leaked. Thus, HR professionals are in an excellent position to prevent cyberthreats (Yoh.com, 2021). There are few things HR leaders can do to minimize a potential breach, maximize the potential for recovery after a breach, and also to maintain the highest level of security for their current and future workforce. One way is to identify an organization's risk exposure, and the first step to preventing threats is recognizing them. Regular assessments help establish what risky employee behaviors can expose an organization to data breaches or other threats. A risk assessment by HR can help an organization discover an unsecured workstation. It can also reveal whether employees have misplaced their ID cards. Risk assessments also help organizations customize their training modules. It can be challenging to provide the right kind of employee training if you don't know what threats your organization could be vulnerable to, making risk assessments even more vital.

Another way is to assure that employee data controls and access restrictions are applied to your systems. There are a variety of ways to protect sensitive data. One of them is putting in place different access controls to this information. A good data management strategy needs access controls to ensure that only a specific set of people can see or use the data stored on an organization's network. HR can also help in security policy-making which is very important for organiza-tions. Every department, including HR, has a role in making and implementing organizational security policies. This ensures that the firm, its clients, and the workforce are always safe from different threats. HR needs to encrypt all employee files and have policies on how employees can access them. It is also vital for HR to work with a firm's management when employees violate guidelines. They should take part in the investigation and also help press charges against offenders. A very important role of HR is to promote a cybersecurity culture which in a sense is everyone's role. HR is one of the most critical players when it comes to creating and nurturing company culture. This is because it is the first and last employee contact point in every organization. And lastly, the most critical HR role in cybersecurity is to educate employees on cybersecurity. Every organization needs to train its employees on information security regularly. This ensures that employees recognize cybersecurity as a standard business practice and stick to the company's best practices. The HR department has a massive role to play in employee information security training. They need to integrate security pieces of training into new-hire orientations. Through training, employees who have not come across data breaches and hacking can react appropriately. This helps to prevent attacks such as phishing or drastically reduce their risk.

Recruitment and Retention

Attracting cyberprofessionals for the workforce of tomorrow, due to a highly diverse pool of candidates, will require a few adjustments as many offers and opportunities will be available to them. When marketing cybersecurity positions having advocacy duties, in addition to touting the work as interesting and challenging, there should be emphasis on the important service to individuals and society. For example, when recruiting advocates for jobs in the public sector, salaries can seldom compete with those in private industry, so appealing to motivators like a sense of civic duty and national pride may be especially helpful in attracting qualified individuals. Service orientation of the work may also appeal to currently underrepresented populations in the cybersecurity workforce who may perceive cybersecurity as having no social benefit or women who desire a career with a socially motivated purpose (Haney & Lutters, 2019).

The opportunity to work collaboratively with talented, diverse people from multiple disciplines should also be highlighted. This emphasis may counter a lack of awareness of the breadth of opportunities available in security careers and belief that only those with deep technical skills can be successful. The interdisciplinary framing might help attract individuals from other fields who possess important nontechnical skills and unique perspectives and encourage a greater sense of self-efficacy. Additionally, an emphasis on the value of diversity may encourage participation of women and minorities who otherwise may be deterred by the stereotype of a white male, hacker-dominated workforce (Haney & Lutters, 2019). Due to the dynamic nature of cybersecurity, organizational challenges, and human nature, the work of advocates can sometimes be daunting and thankless, requiring perseverance and resilience. In addition, individuals qualified for cybersecurity advocate positions possess a valuable blend of skills (Lapena, 2017), so are in danger of being recruited away by others. Therefore, special emphasis should be placed on their retention.

Recruiting the Cybersecurity Professional

When you have one or more cybersecurity positions to fill, it's only a matter of time before the pressure will start to mount to get someone in the role ASAP. You know you can't just throw anyone in the role. When you consider that the top data breaches in 2018 affected more than 100 million people, finding skilled, experienced, trustworthy talent makes getting cybersecurity recruitment right that much more important (Cybersn, 2022). Having a positive company culture and being active on social media are ways to raise the profile of your company and help with cybersecurity recruitment, but they won't get you more resumes in your inbox like the right job description and a solid network of connections will. There are a few cybersecurity recruitment tips to help you find better talent in less time.

To begin with, focus on where to look. Chances are the best and brightest in cybersecurity are already working at another company. It's why most cybersecurity professionals will tell you they are contacted by recruiters on a near daily basis. To find the right candidate for your cybersecurity post, you will have to be more aggressive than managers hiring in other fields. One tip to consider is to look for skills and not just the degree. One of the biggest mistakes companies make when it comes to cyber-security hiring is immediately eliminating candidates without the required degree. Another thing to consider is to review the job description as one of the most difficult challenges in cybersecurity recruitment is getting the job description right. Often, a company may not even have the right job title, leaving the posting to go unnoticed by candidates.

Improving cybersecurity recruitment begins with acknowledging that it's different from filling other jobs. The specialized skill set and high level of trust required makes finding the right talent more difficult. By adopting these approaches, however, you can start to attract better talent faster.

Retaining the Cybersecurity Professional

The tangible and intangible costs of finding and onboarding a single qualified cybersecurity professional can be daunting and quite expensive. To have that employee work for 3 months and then leave for a competitor with a better offer can be just heartbreaking. The goal is to retain that employee for as long as you can and to have them grow and to learn about your organization which in turn keeps your organization safer because they can better protect you. Keep in mind that you are not alone and to what level can be seen in ISACA's 2020 State of Cybersecurity report.

ISACA's 2020 State of Cybersecurity report finds that enterprises are short-staffed, have difficulty identifying enough qualified talent for open positions and don't believe their HR teams adequately understand their hiring needs. Additionally, while slight progress is reported in the effort to increase the number of women in cybersecurity roles and in established diversity programs, most cybersecurity teams still indicate they have significantly more men than women, and most report that progress is minimal (ISACA, 202). "Cybersecurity jobs are in huge demand but, as many organizations are all too aware, it continues to be a real struggle to find the right candidates with the right skills and experience to meet the demands of these roles," says retired Brigadier General Greg Touhill, ISACA board director, and President of the AppGate Federal Group. Some key findings from the report include:

- 62% say their organization's cybersecurity team is under-staffed, and 57% say they currently have unfilled cyberse-curity positions on their team.

- 70% say that fewer than half of their cybersecurity appli-cants are well qualified.

- 72% of cybersecurity professionals believe their HR departments do not regularly understand their needs.

- 58% of respondents anticipate an increase in cybersecurity budgets, an increase of three percentage points from last year, but less than the 64% reported two years ago, signaling that spending may be leveling out.

Survey respondents expressed that having a degree does not necessarily indicate that a candidate is ready for the job, with only 27% saying that recent graduates in cybersecurity are well prepared. They also indicated that candidates are not measuring up in either technical or soft skills, citing as the top five skills gaps being:

- Soft skills (32%)

- IT knowledge and skills gaps (30%)

- Insufficient business insight (16%)

- Cybersecurity technical experience (13%)

- Insufficient hands-on training (10%).

However, when asked about the factors they consider when determining if a cybersecurity candidate is qualified, they place emphasis on technical skills, ranking the top three qualifications as hands-on cybersecurity experience (95%), credentials (89%), and hands-on training (81%).

Once teams achieve the difficult task of finding the right professionals, they then struggle to retain them, with 66% saying it's difficult to retain cybersecurity talent, a slight increase from last year. They cite the main reasons for staff leaving as:

- Recruitment by other companies (59%)

- Limited promotion and development opportunities (50%)

- Poor financial incentives (50%)

- High work stress levels (40%, a 10-percentage point increase from the year prior)

- Lack of management support (39%).

There are seven industry recommendations to aid in retention, foster advocate motivation, and encourage progression of current professionals into advocate roles. These recommendations may be found in Table 8.

CURRENT CYBERSECURITY JOB TITLES

Entry-Level Cybersecurity Jobs

The cybersecurity workforce of tomorrow will be meeting the challenges of the day with KSAs as discussed in the NICE Cybersecurity Framework. However, those KSAs transform into very specific job titles where those KSAs will be used in a daily manner. In the context of cybersecurity, "entry-level" can be a bit of a misnomer. For some roles, the National Security Agency (NSA) defines entry-level as requiring a bachelor's degree plus up to three years of relevant experience and even less with higher-level degrees. With a high school diploma or GED, you'll likely need between four and seven years of relevant experience on your resume to enter the workforce. Most cybersecurity professionals enter the field after gaining experience in an entry-level IT role. Here are a few of the most common entry-level jobs within the bigger world of cybersecurity. Table 9 includes various entry and midlevel cybersecurity jobs, their descriptions, and average salaries.

Table 8. Recommendations to Aid in Retention.

Industry Retention Recommendations

1   Learn to recognize those who are doing advocacy work within the organization, even if in the background. Offer sincere praise and feedback about their successes (even if minor) and tout their mix of technical and nontechnical skill. Provide opportunities to assume more responsibility for security promotion activities.

2   Provide ample opportunity for advocates to receive direct feedback from their audience (face-to-face especially) about their efforts. Implement mechanisms to measure effectiveness and value of advocacy approaches.

3   Support advocates in trying innovative approaches.

4   Encourage advocates to participate in collaborative and information sharing opportunities with others working in related areas.

5   Clearly communicate to the workforce that advocates are supported by leadership as important contributors in protecting people, systems, and information.

6   Arm advocates with professional development and continuous learning opportunities that can aid them in their jobs. This learning should address the interdisciplinary nature of cybersecurity and include organizational, social, and technical aspects of cybersecurity.

7   Be cautious with offering excessive extrinsic incentives as these may interfere with intrinsic motivation. However, try to promote and pay advocates commensurate with the value they bring to the organization. If that is not possible, provide advocates with clear feedback about the importance and value of their work.

Source: Table original creation but content from http://sigmis.org/ CPR2019Program.pdf https://dl.acm.org/doi/proceedings/10.1145/3322385.

Table 9. Entry and Mid-Level Cybersecurity Jobs.

#	Position	Feeder Role	Average Salary	Description	Common Certifications
1	Information security analyst	Network or systems administrator	$99,275	• Monitoring networks for security breaches • Investigating, documenting, and reporting security breaches • Researching IT security trends • Helping computer users with security products and procedures • Developing strategies to help their organization remain secure	CompTIA Security+, GIAC Certified Intrusion Analyst (GCIA), GIAC Certified Incident Handler (GCIH)
2	Information security specialist	Networking, IT support, systems engineering	$97,273	• Testing and maintaining firewalls and antivirus software • Implementing security training • Researching new security risks • Suggesting improvements for security weaknesses	Common certifications: CompTIA Security+, Systems Security Certified Practitioner (SSCP), GIAC Security Essentials (GSEC)

| 3 | Digital forensic examiner | IT support, risk analyst | $75,265 | • Collecting, preserving, and analyzing digital evidence
• Recovering data from erased or damaged hard drives
• Documenting the data retrieval process and maintaining chain of custody
• Assisting law enforcement in criminal investigations
• Providing expert testimony in court proceedings | GIAC Certified Forensic Analyst, EnCase Certified Examiner (EnCE), AccessData Certified Examiner (ACE) |
| 4 | IT auditor | Network administrator, risk analyst, IT support | $79,709 | • Planning and performing audits
• Documenting and presenting audit findings
• Providing guidance on recommended and mandatory security measures
• Designing plans to fix any security risks
• Identifying opportunities for better efficiency | Certifications: Certified Internal Auditor (CIA), Certified Information Systems Auditor (CISA) |

Table 9. (*Continued*)

#	Position	Feeder Role	Average Salary	Description	Common Certifications
5	Security systems administrator	Systems administrator, information security analyst	$108,33	• Monitoring systems and running regular backups • Managing individual user accounts • Developing and documenting security procedures for the organization • Collaborating with security teams to respond to unwanted intrusions • Participating in company-wide security audits	Certified Information Systems Security Professional (CISSP), Certified Information Security Manager (CISM)
6		Information security analyst, incident responder	$106,67	• Planning, designing, and carrying out penetration tests • Creating reports on test results and offering recommendations to security decision-makers	Certified Ethical Hacker (CEH), CompTIA PenTest+, GIAC Certified Penetration Tester (GPEN)

| 7 | Security engineer | Information security analyst, penetration tester | $111,691 | • Developing scripts to automate parts of the testing process
• Conducting social engineering exercises (attempting to get company employees to disclose confidential information)
• Providing technical support during incident handling | • Developing security standards and best practices
• Recommending security enhancements to management
• Ensuring new security systems are installed and configured correctly
• Testing security solutions
• Leading incident response teams
• Developing programs to automate vulnerability detection | Certified Information Systems Security Professional (CISSP), Certified Cloud Security Professional (CCSP) |

Table 9. (*Continued*)

#	Position	Feeder Role	Average Salary	Description	Common Certifications
8	Security architect	Security engineer, information security analyst	$153,751	• Building and maintaining security networks and systems • Preparing budgets and overseeing security expenses • Coordinating security operations across IT and engineering departments • Improving systems in response to security incidents or vulnerabilities • Conducting breach of security drills	Certified Information Systems Security Professional (CISSP), Certified Information Security Manager (CISM), CSA Certificate of Cloud Security Knowledge (CCSK)
9	Cryptography engineer	Computer programmer, information security analyst, systems administrator	$90,529	• Developing new cryptographic algorithms • Analyzing existing algorithms for vulnerabilities • Implementing encryption solutions • Testing new encryption techniques and tools	Certifications: EC-Council Certified Encryption Specialist (ECES)

| 10 | Cybersecurity manager | Information security analyst, security administrator | $132,180 | • Managing human and technological resources
• Tracking changes to internal and external security policy
• Ensuring compliance with security rules and regulations
• Sourcing cybersecurity tools for the organization
• Leading risk mitigation efforts | Certified Information Systems Security Professional (CISSP), Certified Information Security Manager (CISM) |

Source: Table original creation but data from https://www.coursera.org/articles/cybersecurity-jobs.

EXPERT OPINION: MARK AGOVINO, PRESIDENT & CEO, COPPERTREE STAFFING

There is a clear and obvious gap between the demand from organizations for skilled cybersecurity professionals and the available trained and experienced cybersecurity candidates who have both an expansive information technology background and a security focused background based on those technologies. Cybersecurity workers are not just skilled in cybersecurity techniques, but they have an in-depth understanding of the six-component IT framework including Hardware, Software, Data, People, Processes, and Telecommunications. Companies that are looking to hire cybersecurity workers are looking for candidates with several years of dedicated cybersecurity fieldwork with an established information technology background and training. One of the reasons for this is that when a company hires a new graduate, for example, and provides them with both inhouse and possibly professional cybersecurity training, then they become highly desirable on the marketplace and thus more difficult for the hiring organization to retain that employee. In many instances, this is not the actions or efforts of the cybersecurity employee as they are usually genuinely appreciative of the opportunity; however, once these employees update their LinkedIn accounts or GitHub accounts, for example, with new skills and experience, then it becomes extremely difficult for the employee to reject very lucrative offers (they are being found by AI engines) and even more difficult for the original hiring company to retain that employee with respect to salary and benefits but also because they now have thousands of dollars in training costs invested as well.

Some of the retention challenges may be due to companies not implementing well-communicated employee growth plans based on years of services, training acquired, benefits, values of benefits etc. specific to cybersecurity employees, and this makes the employee a target for competing organizations that may be paying top dollar due to an immediate need for a skilled cybersecurity employee. Some forward-thinking companies are now operating internal "universities" to make sure that their workforce is learning everything they need to know to become more efficient, and this includes cybersecurity training and cyberskills training. These programs are sometimes tied to corporate growth and advancement programs that benefit the employee and keep them tied to the organization helping with retention.

Organizations still feel that new graduates are very difficult to hire because they do not possess, nor can they demonstrate, the hands-on skills they need at the time of hiring. It is acknowledged that students are now getting dedicated cybersecurity degrees instead of getting an IT degree and transitioning or even falling into cybersecurity, but there is still the general consensus that students coming out of school are not, in general, demonstrating the practical, hands-on cybersecurity skills needed on day one of the job. This could be that students are learning of the workforce gap and making the transmission of majors and programs based on this gap, but they are still having trouble entering the workforce due to the lack of hands-on experience.

CASE-BASED SCENARIO

In April 2019, it was revealed that two datasets from Facebook apps had been exposed to the public internet. The information related to more than 530 million Facebook users and included phone numbers, account names, and Facebook IDs. However, two years later (April 2021) the data were

posted for free, indicating new and real criminal intent surrounding the data. In fact, given the sheer number of phone
numbers impacted and readily available on the dark web as a
result of the incident, security researcher Troy Hunt added
functionality to his HaveIBeenPwned (HIBP) breached
credential checking site that would allow users to verify if
their phone numbers had been included in the exposed dataset. "I'd never planned to make phone numbers searchable,"
Hunt wrote in a blog post. "My position on this was that it
didn't make sense for a bunch of reasons. The Facebook data
changed all that. There's over 500 million phone numbers but
only a few million email addresses so more than 99% of
people were getting a miss when they should have gotten a
hit." As a thought experiment, discuss with your colleagues
and associates the varying perspectives and points of view of
this Facebook breach from the perspective of the cybercriminal and the cyberhero. Ask yourselves the following questions
and discuss your viewpoints. What methods did the cybercriminal use to attain the Facebook data? How could a
cyberhero have prevented the theft in the first place? Does the
cybercriminal consider the acquisition of phone records theft?
Does the cyberhero consider the acquisition of phone records
theft? Why do they have differing viewpoints? What were the
motivating factors behind the cybercriminals' actions to steal
the data? Why did he not sell the data and only decide to post
it? Was it a criminal who posted the data or just an irre-
sponsible employee?

4

CYBERSECURITY PRODUCTS AND SERVICES

THE CYBERSECURITY TOOLBOX

The cybersecurity workforce of tomorrow will be engaging in a world of regular and organized cybercrime and will have access to a "Cyber Mall" of products and toolsets each of which is designed to perform specific tasks and functionalities. In this chapter we discuss the current and future environment of products and services that the cybersecurity professional will need to navigate, acquire, learn, and implement and sometimes during times of great intensity and strain due to the seriousness and importance of the specific threat at hand.

THE CYBERSECURITY TOOLBOX OF TODAY

There are a variety of software and hardware tools, products, and services that cybersecurity professionals use, but the specific job that probably uses the widest array of unique tools is the cybersecurity analyst as they need to identify, isolate, and sometimes repair or mitigate the specific threats or anomalies identified. Cybersecurity analysts use a variety of tools in their jobs, which can be organized into a few categories including network security monitoring, encryption, web vulnerability, penetration testing, antivirus software, network intrusion detection, and packet sniffers. In the next section we discuss each in more detail.

Network security monitoring tools are used to analyze network data and detect network-based threats. Product examples of these tools include Argus, Nagios, Pof, Splunk, and OSSEC. Encryption tools protect data by scrambling text so that they are unreadable to unauthorized users. Some examples of these tools include Tor, KeePass, VeraCrypt, NordLocker, AxCrypt, and TrueCrypt. Web vulnerability scanning tools are software programs that scan web applications to identify security vulnerabilities including cross-site scripting, SQL injection, and path traversal. Some examples of these tools include Burp Suite, Nikto, Paros Proxy, and SQLMap. Penetration testing, also known as pen testing, simulates an attack on a computer system in order to evaluate the security of that system. Example products of penetration testing tools include Metasploit, Kali Linux, Netsparker, and Wireshark. Antivirus software is designed to find viruses and other harmful malware, including ransomware, worms, spyware, adware, and Trojans, and examples of these tools include Norton 360, Bitdefender Antivirus, Norton AntiVirus, Kaspersky Anti-Virus, and McAfee Total Protection.

Additional products and tools include network intrusion detection systems (NIDS) or IDS monitor network and system traffic for unusual or suspicious activity and notify the administrator if a potential threat is detected. Examples of these systems are Snort, Security Onion, SolarWinds Security Event Manager, Kismet, and Zeek. Packet sniffers or packet analyzers, protocol analyzers or network analyzers are used to intercept, log, and analyze network traffic and data. Examples of these tools include Wireshark, Tcpdump, and Windump. Firewall tools stop data from entering your network based on filters and rules. Product and service examples include Tufin,

AlgoSec, FireMon, and RedSeal. And finally, managed detection vendor services that analyze and proactively detect and eventually eliminate cyberthreats. Alerts are investigated to determine if any action is required.

Network and Packet Analysis

Packet analysis is a primary traceback technique in network forensics, which, providing that the packet details captured are sufficiently detailed, can play back even the entire network traffic for a particular point in time (Leslie F. Sikos). This can be used to find traces of nefarious online behavior, data breaches, unauthorized website access, malware infection, and intrusion attempts, and to reconstruct image files, documents, email attachments, etc. sent over the network. This chapter is a comprehensive survey of the utilization of packet analysis, including deep packet inspection (DPI), in network forensics, and provides a review of artificial intelligence (AI)-powered packet analysis methods with advanced network traffic classification and pattern identification capabilities. Considering that not all network information can be used in court, the types of digital evidence that might be admissible are detailed. The properties of both hardware appliances and packet analyzer software are reviewed from the perspective of their potential use in network forensics.

Virus and Malware Protection

Antivirus software is created specifically to help detect, prevent, and remove malware (malicious software). It is used to prevent, scan, detect, and delete viruses from a computer. Once installed, most antivirus software runs automatically in the background to provide real-time protection against virus attacks. Comprehensive virus protection programs help protect your files and hardware from malware such as worms, Trojan horses, and spyware and may also offer additional protection such as customizable firewalls and website blocking. Antivirus software is a program or set of programs that are designed to prevent, search for, detect, and remove software viruses, and other malicious software like worms, Trojans, adware, and more. These antivirus tools are critical for users to have installed and up-to-date because a computer without antivirus software protection will be infected within minutes of connecting to the internet. The bombardment is constant, which means antivirus companies have to update their detection tools regularly to deal with the more than 60,000 new pieces of malware created daily.

These systems function by protecting your computer and underlying system by detecting, blocking, and removing viruses, malware, and ransomware, preventing identity theft and block phishing and fraud, warning about dangerous websites and links before you click, scanning the dark web to find if an email address has been compromised, keeping online accounts protected with secure password encryption, providing simple training to teach you and your family how to be even safer online, and tuning up your computer to keep it running smoothly. Many antivirus software programs still download malware definitions straight to your device and scan your files in search of matches.

Intrusion Detection

An IDS is a device or software application that monitors a network for malicious activity or policy violations. Any malicious activity or violation is typically reported or collected centrally using a security information and event management system. Some IDSs are capable of responding to detected intrusion upon discovery. These are classified as intrusion prevention systems (IPSs) (Barracude.com, 2021). There is a wide array of IDS, ranging from antivirus software to tiered monitoring systems that follow the traffic of an entire network. The most common classifications are NIDSs and host-based intrusion detection systems (HIDSs). Modern net-worked business environments require a high level of security to ensure safe and trusted communication of information between various organizations. An IDS acts as an adaptable safeguard technology for system security after traditional technologies fail. Cyberattacks will only become more sophisticated, so it is important that protection technologies adapt along with their threats.

Perimeter Security

Perimeter security in cybersecurity refers to the process of defending a company's network boundaries from hackers, intruders, and other unwelcome individuals (Secur-ityforward.com, 2022). This entails surveillance detection, pattern analysis, threat recognition, and effective response. Each private network is surrounded by a perimeter. It serves as a secure wall between networks, such as your company's private intranet and the public internet. A network perimeter includes solutions such as IDSs, IPSs, Firewalls, Border routers, and Unified Threat Management (UTM) systems.

Penetration Testing

A penetration test, also called a pen test or ethical hacking, is a cybersecurity technique organizations use to identify, test, and highlight vulnerabilities in their security posture. These penetration tests are often carried out by ethical hackers. These resident employees or consultants mimic the strategies and actions of an attacker in order to evaluate the vulnerability of an organization's computer systems, network, or web applications. Organizations can also use pen testing to test their adherence to compliance regulations. Kali Linux is a Linux distribution that contains its own collection of hundreds of software tools specifically tailored for their target users which are penetration testers and other security professionals. It also comes with an installation program to completely set up Kali Linux as the main operating system on any computer. This is pretty much like all other existing Linux distributions, but there are other features that differentiate Kali Linux, many of which are tailored to the specific needs of penetration testers. A sample list of Kali Linux pen testing tools can be seen in Table 10, and the full list of Kali tools can be found in the resources section of this book.

Intrusion Prevention Systems

IPSs are control systems that allow or reject data packets based on a predefined set of criteria that is updated regularly or automatically by your managed service provider (MSP). Compared to a standard IDS, which alerts administrators and MSPs to potential threats, IPSs might include an automatic defense mechanism that prevents data from accessing the network without human intervention.

Table 10. Sample List of Kali Linux Tools.

Name	Description	Category
0d1n	Web security tool to make fuzzing at HTTP inputs, made in C with libCurl.	Webapp fuzzer scanner
0trace	A hop enumeration tool.	Scanner
3proxy	Tiny free proxy server.	Proxy
3proxy-win32	Tiny free proxy server.	Windows proxy
42zip	Recursive Zip archive bomb.	Dos
a2sv	Auto Scanning to SSL Vulnerability (HeartBleed, CCS Injection, SSLv3 POODLE, FREAK, LOGJAM attack, SSLv2 DROWN etc).	Scanner
abcd	ActionScript ByteCode disassembler.	Disassembler
abuse-ssl-bypass-waf	Bypassing WAF by abusing SSL/TLS ciphers.	Webapp fuzzer
acccheck	A password dictionary attack tool that targets windows authentication via the SMB protocol.	Cracker
Ace	Automated Corporate Enumerator. A simple yet powerful VoIP Corporate Directory enumeration tool that mimics the behavior of an IP Phone in order to download the name and extension entries that a given phone can display on its screen interface.	Voip
aclpwn	Active Directory ACL exploitation with BloodHound.	Exploitation

Source: Table original creation – data from https://www.kali.org/tools/.

Firewalls

A firewall is a filtering mechanism with a specified set of rules for allowing and restricting traffic from the public network to access the private network and vice versa. It's additional security that guards a company's network against malicious packets of data that may disguise risks.

Border Routers

These are routers that manage traffic into and out of networks. Border routers are the final routers on a company's private network before traffic connects to public internet networks.

Unified Threat Management Systems

By merging the functionalities of IDS and IPS systems, UTM solutions defend the network. From a single point on the private network, a single security device performs numerous security activities. Information entering a company's network is safeguarded by antivirus, antispyware, antispam, firewall, and virtual private network (VPN) features. A UTM system guards against viruses, malware, hacking attempts, and harmful attachments through DPI. DPI examines data transmitted across the network in detail, both inside and out, and analyzes for compliance violations such as Trojans, spam, viruses, or other set criteria. When it detects such infractions, it prevents the data from being received or transferred.

Secure Software Design

The Secure Software Development Framework (SSDF) is a set of fundamental, sound, and secure software development practices based on established secure software development practice documents from organizations such as BSA, OWASP, and SAFECode (Souppaya, Scarfone, & Dodson, 2021). Few software development life cycle (SDLC) models explicitly address software security in detail, so practices like those in the SSDF need to be added to and integrated with each SDLC implementation. Following the SSDF practices should help software producers reduce the number of vulnerabilities in released software, reduce the potential impact of the exploitation of undetected or unaddressed vulnerabilities, and address the root causes of vulnerabilities to prevent recurrences. Also, because the SSDF provides a common language for describing secure software development practices, software producers and acquirers can use it to foster their communications for procurement processes and other management activities.

THE CYBERSECURITY TOOLBOX OF TOMORROW

The cybersecurity workforce of tomorrow will be enveloped in the concept of digital trust and implementing solutions that inherently know who to trust and what resources, and only those resources, they are allowed to see and change based on their authority on that global network.

Technology is key to improving digital trust across an organization's people, process, governance, and regulations. But with the cybersecurity industry filing at least 2,000 patents supporting digital trust between 2015 and 2020, it can be challenging for organizations to determine which tools they need today and tomorrow. Four leading technologies can help improve digital trust. Two of them, AI-based data monitoring and cloud-enabled data trusts, are increasingly well established; two emerging technologies, blockchain and quantum, will likely disrupt digital trust in the years ahead (Deloitte, 2022).

AI-Based Data Monitoring

When an organization is using trust measurement and monitoring tools, leaders can make the strategic decisions that help them improve trust. That's critical to growth: a flawed data model can severely compromise outcomes. But the traditional time-consuming methods of manually identifying and cleaning incorrect, stale, missing, or poorly labeled data cost organizations an average of $13 million annually, according to Gartner. AI can help validate data accuracy, authenticity, and reliability by uncovering missing data, anomalies, or unexpected data in real time, including fake or manipulated documents, images, and even deepfake videos, whose inaccurate shadows and reflections and biometric irregularities may evade manual examination. Similarly, AI can help improve identity and access management, spotting unauthorized access or abnormal user behavior to block bot accounts, and prevent phishing attempts and social engineering or ransomware attacks. Organizations with fully deployed AI solutions can have up to 80% lower cost impacts from data breach incidents than those without, according to IBM. From patient health to user interests, AI can help ensure data are used as intended, flagging intellectual property of various media to identify copyright infringements. AI innovations related to digital trust are growing briskly, and more mature and automated AI solutions are expected to proliferate.

Cloud-Enabled Data Trusts

An organization has no more powerful asset in its possession than its data and no asset in more urgent need of defense. As a bank stores and manages customers' financial assets, an independent third-party data trust governs, controls, and secures data usage and manages legal data rights for authorized parties. Data trusts are integral components of such use cases as engineering smart cities and securing sensitive health or financial data. Given the immense volume of incoming internet of things (IoT) data, data trusts can often be invaluable in helping organizations validate single sources of reliable information, making data management more seamless and adding a layer of privacy, and elevating brand reputations by increasing transparency and reducing both data silos and the risks of breaches or loss.

Blockchain

One technology that first originated in a white paper in 2008 (Nakamoto, 2008) and is primarily known for its use in cryptocurrencies is blockchain. Blockchain is an important technology for the future of cybersecurity based on its level of security due to its powerful encryption methods and its generally accepted immutability and continued research and commercialization may ultimately lead to the technology being widely used in other databases and file storage structures outside of cryptocurrencies. Blockchain technology has recently been used for cybersecurity due to the robustness and integrity preserving nature of its design. Securing Internet of Vehicles (IoV) through blockchain techniques such as security, privacy, reputation, distributed, decentralized, data sharing, authentication, and trust-based approaches (Kumar et al., 2021).

As an overview, blockchain is a distributed database or ledger that is shared among the nodes of a computer network. As a database, a blockchain stores information electronically in digital format. The innovation with a blockchain is that it guarantees the fidelity and security of a record of data and generates trust without the need for a trusted third party. One key difference between a typical database and a blockchain is how the data are structured.

A blockchain collects information together in groups, known as blocks, that hold sets of information. Blocks have certain storage capacities and, when filled, are closed and linked to the previously filled block, forming a chain of data known as the blockchain (Hayes, 2023). All new information that follows that freshly added block is compiled into a newly formed block that will then also be added to the chain once filled. This data structure inherently makes an irreversible timeline of data when implemented in a decentralized nature. When a block is filled, it is set in stone and becomes a part of this timeline. Each block in the chain is given an exact time-stamp when it is added to the chain.

Given its innovative and transformative potential to support digital trust and safety, blockchain technology should be on every organization's radar as a tool to help organizations authenticate identity, establish asset ownership, and automate trust. An independently verifiable, immutable, trusted digital ledger that preserves records of all contracts, transactions, and digital identities, blockchain is already widely recognized as the mechanism that establishes asset ownership for cryptocurrencies and nonfungible tokens (NFTs). Blockchain also permits unprecedented public transparency and authentication to help verify individuals' identities in elections, display the provenance of published news sources, protect against piracy and counterfeiting of materials, and speed legal agreements and financial deals. And as a trusted, continually auditable platform, blockchain can reduce the complexity and risks an organization must endure when working with a vast network of trusted third parties.

Quantum Technologies

Organizations should keep an eye on the emerging and immensely powerful potential of quantum computing poised to disrupt digital trust both for good and for ill. While potentially helping organizations perform vast data analytics to uncover trends and anomalies along with enhancing data encryption systems, it also introduces the threat of exposing data and transactions to cybercrime through the cracking of common encryption techniques. Quantum key distribution (QKD) uses quantum mechanics to distribute encryption keys between two parties, and its tamper-evident properties reveal any attempts at eavesdropping. QKD's limitations, including its complex processes, oversized special equipment, and high costs, have impeded more widespread adoption. Digital trust will depend on organizations implementing post quantum cryptography (PQC): quantum-resistant techniques using mathematical problems too complex for quantum computers to solve. The National Institute of Standards and Technology (NIST) aims to standardize quantum-resistant algorithms by 2024, potentially making PQC more cost-effective and strengthening digital trust by pushing more organizations to improve data hygiene.

Data Science and Big Data Analytics

The cybersecurity workforce of tomorrow will be considering data in every aspect of cybersecurity, and the set of tools used to manipulate that data into some sort of useable and actionable knowledge is known as data science, more specifically cybersecurity data science. In a computing context, cybersecurity is undergoing massive shifts in technology and its operations in recent days, and data science is driving the change. Extracting security incident patterns or insights from cybersecurity data and building corresponding data-driven models is the key to make a security system automated and intelligent.

To understand and analyze the actual phenomena with data, various scientific methods, machine learning (ML) techniques, processes, and systems are used, which is commonly known as data science. In cybersecurity data science, the data are gathered from relevant cybersecurity sources, and the analytics complement the latest data-driven patterns for providing more effective security solutions. The concept of cybersecurity data science allows making the computing process more actionable and intelligent as compared to traditional ones in the domain of cybersecurity (Sarker et al., 2020). The ultimate goal of cybersecurity data science is data-driven intelligent decision-making from security data for smart cybersecurity solutions. CDS represents a partial paradigm shift from traditional well-known security solutions such as firewalls, user authentication and access control, cryptography systems etc. that might not be effective according to today's need in the cyber industry (Anwar et al., 2017).

EXPERT OPINION: MICHAEL GLUCKMAN, CISSP PRESIDENT (ISC)² LONG ISLAND CHAPTER

The ever increasing transition away from brick and mortar businesses moving toward more and more online services is driving the increase in the amount of digital data and most recently, data that are stored on centrally hosted cloud environments. This is because organizations are moving away from the traditional and costly model of hosting their own platforms and computer networks in-house. This increase in centralized data makes it more inviting for cybercriminals to target large central repositories and conversely the amount of data makes it more attractive for organizations to implement more complex tool sets that use AI and ML technologies to learn from the data and make better and more informed decisions at the executive levels. In brick and mortar companies and organizations, there could be a perimeter security strategy in place that could focus on keeping out anyone that's not part of the organization completely outside the perimeter and anyone that is part of the organization and inside the perimeter could access resources on the network. Now with shared services and more than one company storing and sharing data on a single server in a cloud environment it is more important than ever to protect the organization's resources as the data become more available and thus exposed in a cloud or hosted environment.

AI and ML technologies are being used to test new software applications and version releases for new and previously unknown vulnerabilities by cybercriminals, and they are becoming more advanced at this technique every day. For this reason, it is very important for organizations to embrace the use of AI and ML technologies either in use by their cybersecurity vendors or even in technology skills attained and acquired by their own employees as they continue to implement innovative approaches to threat identification and vulnerability analysis. The in-depth knowledge of AI and ML algorithms will not be a mandatory requirement in the future by organizations that are implementing black box security technologies and using services provided by cybersecurity vendors; however, those companies providing those original proprietary vendor services capitalizing on AI and ML technologies will definitely be looking for individuals with very practical and hands-on skills in this area.

Cybersecurity workers of the future will need to have a broad knowledge of information technology and the six-component framework including Hardware, Software, Data, People, Procedures, and Telecommunications, the available security controls, and how to use them, but also of the governance frameworks that drive the requirements for how systems are to be secured at all levels. The cybersecurity workforce of the future will need to have experience with the core technologies that store and transfer valuable data and then the security technologies that protect the data throughout those networks.

CASE-BASED SCENARIO

Hotel Marriot International announced the exposure of sensitive details belonging to half a million Starwood guests following an attack on its systems in September 2018. In a statement published in November the same year, the hotel giant stated that on September 8, 2018, Marriott received an alert from an internal security tool regarding an attempt to access the Starwood guest reservation database. They stated that Marriott quickly engaged leading security experts to help determine what occurred. Marriott learned during the investigation that there had been unauthorized access to the Starwood network since 2014. Marriott recently discovered that an unauthorized party had copied and encrypted information and took steps toward removing it. On November 19, 2018, Marriott was able to decrypt the information and determined that the contents were from the Starwood guest reservation database. The data copied included guests' names, mailing addresses, phone numbers, email addresses, passport numbers, Starwood Preferred Guest account information, dates of birth, gender, arrival and departure information, reservation dates, and communication preferences. For some, the information also included payment card numbers and expiration dates, though these were apparently encrypted.

Marriot carried out an investigation assisted by security experts following the breach and announced plans to phase out Starwood systems and accelerate security enhancements to its network. An article by *New York Times* attributed the attack to a Chinese intelligence group seeking to gather data on US citizens. As a thought experiment, discuss with your colleagues and associates how certain technologies, products, and services could have played a role in this breach. Ask yourselves the following questions and discuss your different perspectives. How could a hastily configured IDS contributed to this breach? How could an improperly configured firewall have allowed the attackers to navigate the system inside the security perimeter? How could chaos engineering have helped Marriott to prepare better for such an attack? Could AI and ML solutions have better alerted Marriott of strange system behaviors and anomalies that could have targeted the attackers so they could be removed from the system?

5

PREPARING THE CYBERSECURITY WORKFORCE OF TOMORROW

INTRODUCTION

Naturally, the cybersecurity workforce of tomorrow starts with the students of today. How early those students are exposed to cybersecurity concepts to prepare them for how they will engage with cybersecxurity throughout their lives is still up for debate, but some argue to begin introducing these concepts as early as preschool and kindergarten. For the purposes of this book, we look at the population of the cybersecurity workforce of tomorrow filled with highly capable problem solvers with high technology skill sets and an understanding of the criminal element and the methods and motivating factors for their behaviors. The workforce of the future begins to be operationally prepared beginning in middle school and high school and includes a wide range of formal training including professional certificate programs, 2-year college programs, 4-year college programs and master's degrees. How this future workforce is being prepared and what corporate and government programs are driving these efforts forward is the focus of this chapter.

Educating the Cybersecurity Workforce of Tomorrow

Institutional Frameworks

Although the governance frameworks already discussed so far are for organizations to comply and demonstrate adequate information security controls and policies within their organizations, there are also frameworks that guide educational institutions to maintain the highest standards of cybersecurity education in direct relation to the latest progressions in the cybersecurity industry regarding the needs in the workforce of today and tomorrow. One of the most comprehensive frameworks for guiding cybersecurity education and filling the pipeline between high school and the cybersecurity workforce is the National Initiative for Cybersecurity Education's (NICE) Cybersecurity Workforce Framework (NCWF).

THE NICE CYBERSECURITY
WORKFORCE FRAMEWORK

The National Initiative for Cybersecurity Education (NICE) Cybersecurity Workforce Framework (NICE Framework) is a reference structure that describes the interdisciplinary nature of cybersecurity work. It serves as a fundamental reference resource for describing and sharing information about cybersecurity work and the knowledge, skills, and abilities (KSAs) needed to complete tasks that can strengthen the cybersecurity posture of an organization.

The framework originated from a workforce-based effort that was led by the National Institute for Standards and Technology called the NICE. The NICE effort resulted in a workforce-based framework of seven job categories, 33 specialty areas, and 52 work roles (Newhouse et al., 2017). Both the CAE and NICE programs fill a void to help define curricular expectations in a rapidly emerging area of significant national importance. These frameworks are created to provide an understanding of what cybersecurity is, give detailed lists of cybersecurity-related tasks, and give guidance on what experience is needed in order to complete such tasks. The workforce frameworks that are discussed below are the National Centers of Academic Excellence in Cyber Defense or Cyber Operations Education Programs (CAE-CD/CO), the NCWF, Department of Defense Directive (DoDD) 8570/8140, and the Cybersecurity Industry Model. The frameworks help map specific segments of the industry and what is to be expected of them when it comes to the cyber workforce.

As a common, consistent lexicon that categorizes and describes cybersecurity work, the NICE Framework improves communication about how to identify, recruit, develop, and retain cybersecurity talent. The NICE Framework is a reference source from which organizations or sectors can develop additional publications or tools that meet their needs to define or provide guidance on different aspects of cybersecurity workforce development, planning, training, and education.

As threats that exploit vulnerabilities in our cyberinfrastructure grow and evolve, an integrated cybersecurity workforce must be capable of designing, developing, implementing, and maintaining defensive and offensive cyber strategies. An integrated cybersecurity workforce includes technical and nontechnical roles that are staffed with knowledgeable and experienced people. An integrated cybersecurity workforce can address the cybersecurity challenges inherent to preparing their organizations to successfully implement aspects of their missions and business processes connected to cyberspace.

A user of the NICE Framework will reference it for different aspects of workforce development, education, and/or training purposes, and when that material is used at organizational levels, the user should customize what is pulled from the NICE Framework to standards, regulations, needs, and mission of the user's organization. The NICE Framework is a reference starting point for the content of guidance and guidelines on career paths, education, training, and credentialing programs. The NICE Framework is a resource that will strengthen an organization's ability to communicate consistently and clearly about cybersecurity work and its cybersecurity workforce. Organizations or sectors can develop additional publications or tools that meet their needs to define or provide guidance on different aspects of workforce development, planning, training, and education. The NICE framework includes nine work role categories, 31 specialty areas, and over 1,000 types of knowledge, skills, and abilities. Major categories are described in Table 11.

DoD Directive 8140.01

The Cyberspace Workforce Management directive, DoDD 8140.01 was released on August 11, 2015. This directive is defined for managing workforce development for personnel who support DoD intelligence, security, and law enforcement missions in cyberspace. The goal of this directive is to unify the overall cyberspace workforce and establish specific workforce elements to align, manage, and standardize cyberspace work roles, baseline qualifications, and training requirements.

In June 2014, the U.S. Department of Labor published their own model of cybersecurity competencies as seen in Fig. 12. This model defines the latest skill and knowledge requirements needed by individuals whose activities impact the security of their organization's cyberspace. The purpose of it is to provide a knowledge roadmap to interested citizens who are new to the industry or those with limited experience thus promoting cybersecurity employment and a robust labor force. The

Table 11. Work Role Category.

Categories	Descriptions
Securely Provision (SP)	Conceptualizes, designs, procures, and/or builds secure information technology (IT) systems, with responsibility for aspects of system and/or network development.
Operate and Maintain (OM)	Provides the support, administration, and maintenance necessary to ensure effective and efficient IT system performance and security.
Oversee and Govern (OV)	Provides leadership, management, direction, or development and advocacy so the organization may effectively conduct cybersecurity work.
Protect and Defend (PR)	Identifies, analyzes, and mitigates threats to internal IT systems and/or networks.
Analyze (AN)	Performs highly specialized review and evaluation of incoming cybersecurity information to determine its usefulness for intelligence.
Collect and Operate (CO)	Provides specialized denial and deception operations and collection of cybersecurity information that may be used to develop intelligence.
Investigate (IN)	Investigates cybersecurity events or crimes related to IT systems, networks, and digital evidence.

Source: NIST: Cybersecurity Workforce Framework https://www.nist.gov/itl/applied-cybersecurity/nice/nice-framework-resource-center.

model incorporates many competencies identified in the already mentioned NCWF and intends to complement NCWF by including both the competencies and requirements needed by not only the average worker who uses the internet or an organization's computer network but as well as a cybersecurity professional already in the workforce.

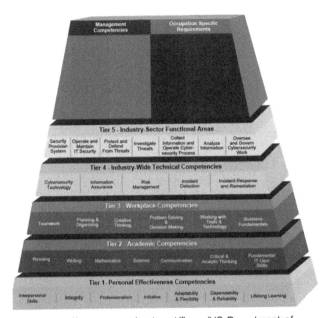

Source: https://www.researchgate.net/figure/US-Department-of-Labor-Employment-and-Training-Administrations-Cybersecurity_fig1_334151137.

Fig. 12. U.S. Department of Labor, Employment and Training Administration's Cybersecurity Competency Model.

The model is part of a general competency clearinghouse maintained by the Employment and Training Administration that is intended to aggregate and clarify industry standards. The stated purpose of this clearinghouse is to provide employers and employment candidates with industry expectations. The model is intentionally broad so that proprietors may add or subtract competencies to fit their own experiences and expectations. The competencies are primarily categorized by tier, with each tier progressively specific to the cybersecurity industry.

Government Drivers of Cybersecurity Education

The current US policy on cybersecurity education, training, awareness, and workforce development is reflected to a large extent by the NICE, led and coordinated by the National Institute of Standards and Technology (NIST), and the National Science Foundation's (NSF's) CyberCorps: Scholarship for Service (SFS) programs, which have worked closely together for years to produce positive outcomes for students and thereby improve cybersecurity for all. Examining cybersecurity changes over the past decade and how they affect everyday life is useful in examining how well programs like NICE align with current challenges. The almost daily reports in the media about cybersecurity breaches and attacks have raised the field's visibility tremendously (Mcduffie & Pitrowski). One of the most productive programs to date has been the CAE-CDE supported and funded by the National Security Agency (NSA) and the DoD.

CAE-CD/CO Program

In the United States, early work in attempting to define the academic parameters of cybersecurity was performed by the NSA through the CAE program, which was first developed and put in place in 1998. Institutions meeting the criteria established by this program are designated as CAE. This program has led the way in establishing content for cybersecurity programs and setting parameters on what a cybersecurity discipline might look like.

The CAE have two education programs called CD and CO which are cosponsored by the NSA and the Department of Homeland Security (DHS). The goal of these education programs is to reduce vulnerability in the national information infrastructure and produce more qualified and trained cyber-security experts coming out of higher education. The purpose of the CAE-CD program is to help strengthen the nation's cyber defenses by "promoting higher education and research in cyber defense and producing professionals with cyber defense expertise." Institutions designated as part of this program must demonstrate outreach, practice of cyber defense at the institution level, and successfully mapping the institution's curriculum to the two-year Core Knowledge Units (KUs). These KUs are displayed in Fig. 13.

Once met, schools receive formal recognition from the US government and may elect to specialize in several possible focus areas. The CAE-CO program complements the CAE-CD program but provides emphasis on tools and techniques used in the cyber world. The CAE-CO is deeply technical and rooted in computer science, computer engineering, and electrical engineering disciplines, with extensive opportunities for hands-on applications in opportunities such as labs and exercises.

DEVELOPING THE CYBERSECURITY WORKFORCE

Based upon the giant deficiency of the cybersecurity talent pool and the severe cyberspace threats, cybersecurity work-force development became the key to assuring that one nation has adequate security measures to protect and defend infor-mation and information systems, and yet, more than 30% of companies are short of security expertise (Liu & Tu, 2020). In 2017, the United States employed nearly 780,000 people in cybersecurity positions, with approximately 350,000 current cybersecurity openings unfilled, according to CyberSeek, a

Knowledge Unit Usage Notional Structure

Centers of Academic Excellence in Cyber Defense Education (CAE-CDE) Designation Requirements

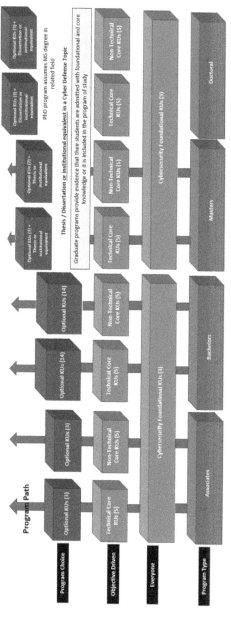

Knowledge Units (KU's)

Foundational: Cybersecurity Foundations, Cybersecurity Principles, and IT Systems Components

Technical Core: Basic Scripting and Programming, Basic Networking, Network Defense, Basic Cryptography, Operating Systems Concepts

Nontechnical Core: Cyber Threats, Policy, Legal, Ethics, and Compliance, Security Program Management, Security Risk Analysis, Cybersecurity Planning and Management

Source: https://dl.dod.cyber.mil/wp-content/uploads/cae/pdf/unclass-cae-cd_ku.pdf.

Fig. 13. Knowledge Unit Usage Notional Structure.

project supported by the NICE, a program of the NIST in the U.S. Department of Commerce.

CYBERSECURITY EDUCATION AT EVERY LEVEL

The cybersecurity workforce of the tomorrow begins to be operationally prepared beginning in middle school and high school and includes a wide range of formal training including professional certificate programs, 2-year college programs, 4-year college programs, and master's degrees. These foundational theory based programs combined with practical hands-on activities and exercises to provide the students with hands-on cybersecurity skills are key to assuring that a regular flow or pipeline of effective cybersecurity professionals are entering the workforce each year. These programs are discussed in the following sections.

Professional Certificates

More than half of all cybersecurity job postings request at least one certification. If you're new to cybersecurity, consider starting with a more foundational certification, like the CompTIA Security+. From there, you can start gaining the necessary work experience to earn more advanced certifications. Professional certificates are one way of both attaining cybersecurity knowledge and expertise while at the same time attaining a recognized certificate of achievement that lets potential employers know that you have the demonstrable skills needed to perform duties for which they have the need. One source for cybersecurity professional certificate information is the National Initiative for Cybersecurity Careers and Studies or NICCS. NICCS' vision is to provide the nation with the tools and resources necessary to ensure the Nation's workforce has the appropriate training and education tools in the cybersecurity field. They also aim to increase awareness of valuable tools and resources available to help educate you during your studies and career. Cybersecurity certifications are valuable for anyone in the cybersecurity space, and NICCS has compiled a list of well-known industry certifications. Some are perfect starting points on your career path and others will help increase future career opportunities. NICCS wants to highlight those certifications in need which will help close the skill gaps in the cybersecurity workforce. Table 12 lists these certifications for further exploration. The table is in alphabetical order and in no way identifies the certificates based on any order of preference.

K-12 Education

According to (Liu & Tu, 2020), 67 out of the 14,832 school districts from 50 states defined cybersecurity courses to offer to K-12 students. It aims to increase student interest in cybersecurity careers, which may, in turn, increase the pipeline of the future cybersecurity workforce. The CAE program, a joint effort between NSA and the higher education community, has accredited less than 250 US higher education institutions as the NSA/DHS designated CAE-CD and certified their cybersecurity programs including 2-year, 4-year, and graduate programs, with a rigorous curriculum that is well mapped to a set of core and optional Cybersecurity KUs. Private sectors have also been actively involved in the cybersecurity education program development, and numerous training and certification programs have been launched. However, these efforts still fall in short to address the huge

Table 12. Professional Certificates in Cybersecurity.

A+

Advanced Security Practitioner

Certified Authorization Professional (CAP)

Certified Cloud Security Professional (CCSP)

Certified Cyber Forensics Professional (CCFP)

Certified Ethical Hacker (CEH)

Certified Expert Penetration Tester (CEPT)

Certified Incident Handler (CIH)

Certified Information Security Manager (CISM)

Certified Information System Auditor (CISA)

Certified Information Systems Security Professional (CISSP)

Certified Penetration Tester (CPT)

Certified Penetration Testing Consultant (CPTC)

Certified Penetration Testing Engineer (CPTE)

Certified Secure Software Lifecycle Professional (CSSLP)

Certified Security Analyst (CSA)

Certified Security Testing Associate (CSTA)

Certified Virtualization Professional (CVP)

CyberSec First Responder (CFR)

HealthCare Information Security and Privacy Practitioner (HCISPP)

Master Mobile Application Developer (MMAD)

Network+

Offensive Security Certified Professional (OSCP)

Security+

Security Essentials Certification (SEC)

Server+

Systems Security Certified Practitioner (SSCP)

national workforce shortage, and more quality academic programs need to be developed.

Community Colleges

Research indicates that the key to developing more graduates in the cybersecurity field is establishing a meaningful pathway in the educational process. Studies have shown that while 46% of undergraduates in the United States are enrolled in community colleges, only 25% of them will transfer to a four-year institution within five years; however, 62% of those transferred will complete a bachelor's degree within six years (Jennifer & Sandy, 2016). These statistics indicate that one of the keys to developing more graduates with a bachelor's degree is to assure more community college students make the transfer. Recent studies have shown that motivation and a well-developed pathway are keys to transferring from a community college to a four-year institution. The course curriculum of cybersecurity programs at different colleges may have varying specializations, and cybersecurity programs at community colleges are usually designed with certification as an endpoint. Hence, gaps exist between 2-year and 4-year cybersecurity programs. One-on-one course mapping between a 2-year program and a 4-year cybersecurity program is not always practical. Currently, program-level articulation agreements between 4-year and 2-year cybersecurity programs are either missing or have become outdated due to the dramatic changes in the course curriculum and plans of study within cybersecurity programs. Hence, there is a critical need to develop a seamless pathway that can motivate students and successfully transition them to a 4-year degree program (Liu & Tu, 2020).

Undergraduate and Graduate Degrees

According to a report by McAfee Burling Glass Technologies, obtaining a bachelor's degree is the minimum qualification for entry-level positions in cybersecurity, with nearly half of companies making it a minimum requirement (Liu & Tu, 2020). This is especially true in the United States that 70% of US companies require a bachelor of science (BS) degree as a minimum requirement. With a large number of prestigious colleges and universities that offer computer science and IT degrees, cybersecurity programs are still less common than traditional computer science degree programs.

Cybersecurity is inherently interdisciplinary at the individual level and multidisciplinary at the team level. The ubiquitous and increasingly complex nature of cyberspace necessarily demands application of expertise in so many disparate disciplines that a single cybersecurity curriculum cannot provide sufficient breadth and depth. The cybersecurity team of the future will require a multidisciplinary team and thus multidisciplinary curricular foundations needed to produce such a team. Although many programs and curricula aspire to a multidisciplinary viewpoint, the current curricular models claiming to support a multidisciplinary perspective primarily integrate notions of other disciplines into an individual one and are, therefore, more interdisciplinary in nature.

CYBERSECURITY JOB ACQUISITION

As in any field that experiences a hiring boom, simply having a degree or certification does not automatically mean that you have a job. There is still a fairly rigorous hiring process that occurs in cybersecurity for a number of reasons. These reasons range from as basic as requiring candidates to have a clean background check to more advanced requirements like assuring that candidates can demonstrate advanced skill sets like network design or packet analysis techniques. Depending on the jobs that are available and that specific job that the candidate is interviewing for, a cybersecurity candidate must be prepared to demonstrate the hands-on techniques and experience that organizations are looking for in a cybersecurity professional but also the problem-solving and analytical resourcefulness to identify problems and come up with potential applicable solutions to solve the problems. While requirements for cybersecurity jobs vary widely from company to company, you might notice some common trends. Let's take a closer look at some of the requirements, and how you can go about meeting them to get your first cybersecurity job.

Educational Requirements

Many jobs in cybersecurity list a bachelor's degree in computer science, information technology, or a related field as a requirement. While degrees are common among professionals in the cybersecurity industry, they're not always required. An $(ISC)^2$ survey of 1,024 cybersecurity professionals in the United States and Canada found that more than half felt that an education in cybersecurity is "nice to have" but not "critical." About 20% of those surveyed with less than three years of experience had only an associate or technical degree $((ISC)^2, 2021)$. Having a bachelor's or master's degree can often create more job opportunities, make you a more competitive candidate in the cybersecurity job market, or help you advance in your career.

EDUCATIONAL TOOLS FOR HANDS-ON PREPARATION

Cybersecurity Sandboxes

Sandboxing is a cybersecurity practice where you run code, observe, and analyze code in a safe, isolated environment on a network that mimics end-user operating environments. Sandboxing is designed to prevent threats from getting on the network and is frequently used to inspect untested or untrusted code. Sandboxing keeps the code relegated to a test environment so it doesn't affect, infect, or cause damage to the host machine or operating system (Checkpoint.com, 2021). As the name suggests, this isolated test environment functions as a kind of "sandbox," where you can play with different variables and see how the program works. This is also a safe space, where if something goes wrong, it can't actively harm your host devices. Sandboxing is an effective way to improve your organization's security, since it's proactive and offers the highest possible threat detection rate. Read more about the benefits of sandboxing below. Sandboxing works by keeping potentially malicious programs or unsafe code isolated from the rest of the organization's environment. This way, it can be analyzed safely, without compromising your operating system or host devices. If a threat is detected, it can be removed proactively.

There are several advantages to using a sandbox including, primarily, that it prevents your host devices and operating systems from being exposed to potential threats and, additionally, can help evaluate potentially malicious software for threats. In addition, you can quarantine and eliminate zero-day threats safely and a sandbox can act as a complementary strategy to your other security products and policies, providing you with even more protection.

Cybersecurity Ranges

According to a report from McAfee, the global cost of cybercrime for 2020 was over one trillion dollars (Smith, Lostri, & Lewis, 2020). Cybersecurity breaches and attacks have not only cost businesses and organizations millions of dollars but have also threatened national security and critical infrastructure. Examples include the ransomware attack in May of 2021 on the largest fuel pipeline in the United States and the February 2021 remote access system breach of a Florida water treatment facility which raised sodium hydroxide to a lethal level. Improving cybersecurity requires a skilled workforce with relevant knowledge and skills. Academic degree programs, boot camps, and various certification programs provide education and training to assist this need. Cyber ranges are a more recent development to provide hands-on skill training. These ranges, often virtual, provide a safe and accessible environment to improve practical skills and experience through hands-on application. They provide a training environment to identify threats, apply countermeasures, and secure data from risks separately from the organization's actual network. More and more academic programs utilize cyber ranges due to the perceived benefit of integrating them into their cybersecurity-related programs. Academic cyber ranges offer virtualized environments that support cybersecurity educators' needs to provide students with a safe, separated, and engaging environment (Beauchamp, 2022).

Cybersecurity Competitions

Cybersecurity competitions are amazing learning opportunities for students and provide an added hands-on experience beyond the labs used in our courses to enhance the knowledge and skills of college graduates. Students who compete in cybersecurity competitions are known to be more desired by industry and government agencies as they are team players and know how to work under time constraints. One of the types of cybersecurity competitions that has been shown to provide the most valuable experiences for students and also for employers seeking candidates are capture-the-flag (CTF) competitions. CTF cyber events are some of the most popular forms of cyber security competitions. In some cyber security circles, successful CTF teams are elevated to the height of sports teams. This is aided by the spectator-friendly nature of CTF events, in which score boards often highlight the number of points held by all of the many teams competing in large rooms (Cybersecuritydegrees.com).

Many students share that challenging CTFs contributed toward the enjoyment of participating, making them a rewarding and worthwhile experience. However, students also feel that academic and team support contributed toward their confidence in competing. In contrast, those who do not report confidence stated they lacked a team strategy or support from their academic institution. Additionally, they did not know what to expect to prepare before the competition event. Overall, the results of this dissertation highlight the importance of prior preparation for educators and student CTF participants. For educators, this prior preparation includes curriculum supporting resources such as content mapping to learning objectives and professional development opportunities that do not assume any prior knowledge or experience. For students, prior preparation includes understanding what to expect and recommendations for academic and team support.

CTF events come in a number of formats. The most popular formats for CTF events, however, are jeopardy, attack–defense, or a mix of the two styles. The jeopardy format involves presenting teams with a wide range of challenge types, similar to the television show *Jeopardy*. Only for each challenge, generally a technical solution is required. Common challenge types may involve networking, reverse engineering, cryptography, hacking, programming, mobile-centered challenges, and forensics challenges.

Table 13 exhibits examples of various cybersecurity competitions.

Cybersecurity Internships and Co-Ops

Research supporting the positive role that experiential learning plays in the career outcomes of college graduates has prompted institutions to consider the internship as an important curricular option (Summit, Platform, Polls, Briefs, & Market, 2017). Despite the controversy over the value of paid versus unpaid internships, recent studies have indicated that students graduating with internship experiences, in general, are more likely than students without those experiences to find employment upon graduation (Callahan & Benzing, 2004; D'Abate, 2010; Gault, Redington, & Schlager, 2000; Knouse, Tanner, & Harris, 1999; Knouse & Fontenot, 2008). Adding to the research, Look Sharp's 2016 State of Millennial Hiring Report indicates that graduates who complete three or more internships are more likely to secure full-time employment, with 81.1% of graduates reporting that the internships helped them shift their career directions either significantly (34.8%) or slightly (46.3%) by changing the focus of classes or majors. Further, Knouse and Fontenot (2008) found that, in addition to having employment opportunities evolve directly from their internship sites upon graduation, interns have enhanced employability after successfully completing their internships even prior to graduation.

Table 13. Cybersecurity Competitions and Challenges.

	Cybersecurity Competition	Competition Description
1	NCCDC: NATIONAL COLLEGIATE CYBER DEFENSE COMPETITION	Started in 2004, the National Collegiate Cyber Defense Competition was established with the aim of providing a template for cyber security organizations at the collegiate level as well as to provide infrastructure for competitions between schools with cybersecurity organizations. Schools sign up for the annual competitions by first joining competition in the geographic region in which they are located. Competition then proceeds from qualifiers, to regional competition, to national competition.
2	PWN2OWN	Pwn2Own is a hacking contest presented annually at the CanSecWest Conference. The contests challenge cybersecurity professionals to find flaws and exploit consumer software and devices. $100,000's in prizes are available annually for contest winners.
3	PWNIUM	Pwnium is presented by Google and often takes place at the same location as Pwn2Own at the CanSecWest Conference. Challenges center around finding vulnerabilities in Chrome OS. In the past, several million dollars in prize money has been available to winning participants.
4	PITCOCTF	PicoCTF is a cybersecurity competition available to middle– and high-school students. The event is put on by Carnegie Mellon University and places teams into an interactive environment and storyline where they must hack, decrypt, reverse engineer, and break different sandbox elements. The competition is the largest cyber security competition available to middle and high schoolers.
5	U.S. CYBER CHALLENGE	The US Cyber Challenge (USCC) is presented by the Center for Internet Security and offers a number of cyber security competitions. Competitions occur online and through the number of summer camps hosted by the USCC organization.

6	DEF CON CONTESTS	Probably the largest cyber security conference, DEF CON presents a wide range of contents that often change from year to year. Common competitions include hacking, lock picking, scavenger hunts, and the highly prestigious capture-the-flag contest. The conference takes place in Las Vegas annually.
7	PANOPLY	Panoply is a network assessment and network defense competition put on by the University of Texas at San Antonio. The timed event is put on at large conferences every year. In the competition, teams accumulate points through controlling and operating critical network resources such as SMTP, DNS, HTTP, HTTPS, or SSH. Throughout the competition, additional resources are added to the common pool that both teams are fighting over, forcing teams to choose between attempting to control new resources or defend existing resources.
8	CSAW CAPTURE THE FLAG (CTF)	The Cyber Security Awareness Week was founded by NYU Tandon Engineering School and is now celebrated around the world. With locations in North America, the Middle East, Europe, and Asia, the event is the largest student-run cyber security event in the world. Part of each year's events include the prestigious capture the flag. Additionally, an applied research competition, embedded security challenge, and policy challenge are present. 2016 saw over 10,000 preliminary competitors at the high school and collegiate levels.
9	NCL: NATIONAL CYBER LEAGUE	The National Cyber League was created in 2011 as an educational and recruiting tool. Every "game" that cyber security students and professionals participate in is built around learning objectives. And for those seeking work, a "scouting report" can give future employers a glimpse of participant technical chops, time management, and ability to deal with pressure. Games are hosted in the "NCL Stadium," a cloud-based environment for competitions throughout an annual "season."

Table 13. (Continued)

	Cybersecurity Competition	Competition Description
10	SANS NETWARS	The SANS Institute offers a series of challenge types through their NetWars modules. These challenges are available for a wide variety of skill levels, and even feature a miniaturized physical city over which challenge participants can attempt to compete for the cyber resources. The annual Tournament of Champions is hosted at the CDI Conference in which those who qualify through winning NetWars competitions face off. A wide range of competitions are available throughout the year in locations around the world.
11	CYBERPATRIOT	CyberPatriot is a program established for the K-12 education of students in cyber security by the Air Force Association. There are three branches of the program, including the National Youth Cyber Defense Competition, AFA CyberCamps, and Elementary School Cyber Education Initiative. The Cyber Defense Competition starts at the state level and then regional level. Top competitors are then given an all-expense paid trip to the national finals in Baltimore, Maryland. At nationals, participants compete for national recognition and scholarship money.
12	MITRE CYBER ACADEMY	Mitre presents its annual STEM Capture-the-Flag challenge that is open to both current students and professionals. While current professionals may compete in the competition for education and training purposes, only eligible high school and college teams will be able to obtain winning prizes, scholarships, and internships. A wide range of other competitions are presented throughout the year by Mitre.

Source: Original Table created with competition data from competition websites.

Cybersecurity Simulation

A significant challenge to maintaining security within an organization is the training of a nontechnical workforce to respond appropriately to cybersecurity threats. Online environments that utilize experiential learning give nontechnical workers an increased exposure to issues in cybersecurity (Burris, Deneke, & Maulding, 2018). A simulation-based approach provides a better understanding of specific cybersecurity threats through experiential learning. Using simulations of cybersecurity threats to provide concrete experiences rather than descriptions in the simulation, the user can attempt multiple actions and is provided with an "awareness" measure. For each, the system provides continuous feedback to allow active experimentation. After each threat has been exposed, the environment provides a narrative of the user's actions with suggested improvements to allow for reflective observation.

EQUALITY IN CYBERSECURITY EDUCATION

Today's technology environment in organizations is far more reactive rather than proactive as it relates to cybersecurity risks and threats (Rogers, 2019). Men dominate the cybersecurity job market. Women make up only 14% of the US cybersecurity workforce (McQuaid & Cervantes, 2019). Developing populations of underdeveloped people into cybersecurity jobs is critical to meeting the workforce shortage.

In the efforts to combat the cyberterrorism crisis, we should explore a much higher crisis – U.S. national unemployment to address significant issues, high urban and rural unemployment potentially, and massive cybersecurity workforce shortages with one creative approach themed oriented charter schools. There is an epidemic of national unemployment within minority groups (Finch et al., 2020). African American and Latino males are experiencing a grave deficit of job opportunities (Muliakal & Issa, 2019). This systemic concern begins at the educational and school level. Studies reflect 45% of Black men in the urban Chicago area within the age of 20–24 that were either in an educational program or working (Muliakal & Issa, 2019). While in other underserved communities, there is an alarming 15.8% unemployment rate in Newark, NJ and 17.4% in Detroit, MI (Perry, 2019). This crisis has caused a national unemployment rate among the African American community, creating a widespread rise of African American men without formal education, jobless, and ill-prepared for twenty-first-century jobs and careers (Muliakal & Issa, 2019). In retrospect, this is a cause for a national emergency to redirect.

THE CYBERSECURITY WORKFORCE OF TOMORROW

The cybersecurity workforce of tomorrow will need to have most of the skill sets and experience we discussed in this book so far but will also need to know how to work in teams. Additionally, there will be specific areas of expertise that will inevitably need to be either attained or learned to become true team members working toward a common cybersecurity goal. The future of cybersecurity holds team-based approaches to organizational security and reduced risk and the team members will need to hold specific skill sets that when compromised as a team create a common and cohesive security-focused engine for the organization. These skills include experience with AI and Data Science, Cognitive Psychology, Operations Research, Electrical and Computer Engineering, Political Science, Knowledge of the Law, Business and Business Management, and the ability to work in multidisciplinary teams. The following sections discuss how each of these apply to the cybersecurity workforce of tomorrow.

AI and Data Science

These experts will play a crucial role on the cybersecurity team, working closely with the computing and operations research professionals to refine and improve their automated tools so that the human–machine defenses and opportunities can be used across all disciplines to combat the ever-increasing automated and intelligent capabilities of adversaries. They will develop, train, update, and evaluate ML recommendation systems that provide the kind of advice and guidance that customers currently get from companies such as Amazon or Netflix. These systems will undoubtedly also be used for numerous other tasks such as quality assurance.

Cognitive Psychology

Cybersecurity cognitive scientists and psychologists will address issues related to human factors, human–machine interfaces and teaming, human behavior, talent assessment, team performance, and team communication. They will also provide explanations for and remove bias from AI, develop effective training materials, and understand human limitations in decision-making. They will create models to analyze workflow and estimate cognitive load as well as predict human behavior.

Operations Research

Operations research includes elements from mathematics, statistics, systems engineering, economics, and computing. These diverse fields will collectively provide professionals with expertise across a vast range of subjects including cryptography, mathematical foundations of what can and cannot be computed in a timely fashion, game theory, project management optimization, ML, and quantum computing. They will play a significant role in evaluating levels of risk as well as simulating and modeling the impact of cybersecurity team solutions based on potential technical and human behaviors. They will work with the AI experts, computing professionals, cognitive scientists, marketing professionals, lawyers, and political scientists to provide valuable, legal, and intelligent use of data analytics.

Electrical and Computer Engineering

Electrical and computer engineers provide expertise on hardware, communications systems, network infrastructure, and photonics. They will develop or ensure the security of everything from chips to hardware components, embedded processes, sensors, drives, controllers, computer architectures, communication systems, and other disciplinary equipment and concepts. In particular, with the increased presence of the Internet of Things (including many sensors and devices within humans), this currently underrepresented domain will be critical.

Political Science

These policy professionals provide a wide variety of expertise in strategy and policy issues, ranging from defense and deterrence to escalation and influence campaigns. They will bring broad knowledge of current and past events, with a clear understanding of the impact of cyber events on people, and on the private and public sectors, as well as the complex interplay between those impacts. They will actively work at understanding what the cybersecurity team is considering doing, describing potential unintended consequences and working with the management and marketing professionals developing internal policies as well as strategies for incentivizing behaviors.

Law

Cybersecurity lawyers provide legal and ethical expertise related to issues involving privacy, security, contracting, intelligence, and surveillance at the local, state, national, and international levels. In military domains, they will possess knowledge on the intersection of cybersecurity with the Law of Armed Conflict, Geneva Conventions, and other issues related to sovereignty and international norms. Cybersecurity lawyers will also provide knowledge and expertise on public–private partnerships and information sharing among various government agencies and the private sector. As in-house counsel, they may, among other things, proactively engage with the team and enterprise about liability, law suits, and intellectual property to ensure that both the cybersecurity solutions/practices and the enterprise services are in compliance, including as products are developed. From inside both government agencies and private companies, they may work to influence and change government policies, laws, and international agreements to facilitate stronger cybersecurity practices for both the public and private sector.

The cybersecurity international relations experts will provide strategy, policy, and cyber threat intelligence expertise at the nation-state level. They will help the team understand how differing values, laws, ethics, and perspectives will impact operations that cross national boundaries. They will be the experts in evaluating and crafting means to influence cultures and their behavior and in understanding how these contribute to cooperation and conflict in cyberspace. They will maintain diplomatic and global security perspectives and help the organization increase trust and cooperation across international boundaries.

Together with the political scientists, international relations experts will work with marketing and management to develop information-sharing policies and partnership practices that facilitate mutually maintaining security and bringing a broader perspective on the full range of levers of national power, how nations use them to coerce or compel one another, and how they can either lead to success or unintended consequences.

Business and Business Management

The impact of cybersecurity is felt throughout the organization. Each of the key departments within a modern corporation such as operations, finance, and marketing, leverage modern information technology systems, with success or failure inextricably linked to cybersecurity. Business specialists will team with computing professionals who may still be learning the business processes of the organization. There is also now a realization that hacking attacks are sometimes a combination of relatively simple security exploits adapted to create public embarrassment or damage. These individuals will lead the efforts to identify such vulnerabilities and prevent such incidents. Depending on the organization, they may be from a mix of professions, such as public affairs and communications, engineers, health professionals, transportation experts, financial wizards, intelligence gatherers, members of the military, or government employees.

Leadership of the cybersecurity team of the future is still an open question. As with chief information officers, it is unclear whether a technical, business, or interdisciplinary background will provide the preponderance of leaders. It is also unknown whether leadership of future cybersecurity teams will evolve from the chief information security officer position and whether it warrants a board-level position. It is clear, however, that leaders of future cybersecurity teams will have to be masters of putting together and mentoring great teams, perhaps in a manner similar to the abilities of general managers and head coaches of successful professional sports teams. Leadership of the cybersecurity team will also work with several other interested parties to facilitate and conduct information sharing, both internal and external to the organization.

CASE-BASED SCENARIO

Over an eight-month period, a developer working for an affiliate marketer scraped customer data, including usernames and mobile numbers, from the Alibaba Chinese shopping website, Taobao, using crawler software that he created. It appears the developer and his employer were collecting the information for their own use and did not sell it on the black market, although both were sentenced to three years in prison. A Taobao spokesperson said in a statement: "Taobao devotes substantial resources to combat unauthorized scraping on our platform, as data privacy and security is of utmost importance. We have proactively discovered and addressed this unauthorized scraping. We will continue to work with law enforcement to defend and protect the interests of our users and partners." As a thought experiment, discuss with your colleagues and associates how the global cybersecurity education system played a role in this breach. Questions for you to consider include: Did the current cybersecurity workforce gap play a role in this breach? Would a steady flow of skilled and talented cybersecurity workers helped to avoid this breach? Does the affinity of organizations to hire only workers with experience degrade the workforce pipeline? How does a high school student that is considering cybersecurity as a career affect this breach from happening in the future? What are the national costs of not establishing a pipeline of cybersecurity workers starting in high school?

FURTHER READING

The Cuckoo's Egg – Clifford Stoll
Often cited as one of the best cybersecurity reads, this 1989 tale depicts Clifford's extensive investigation into a notable cyber-alert.

The Cybersecurity Playbook – Allison Cerra
This is a step-by-step guide to protecting your organization from unknown threats and adopting good security habits for everyday business situations.

Python Crash Course, 2nd Edition – Eric Matthes
The top seller, according to No Starch Press, is this "hands-on, project-based introduction" to the core of Python programming.

Cyber War: The Next Threat to National Security and What to Do about It – Richard A. Clarke and Robert K. Knake
This is the most heavily-reviewed cybersecurity book on Amazon with more than 240 ratings. In this book, Clarke and Knake trace the rise of the cyber-age and profile the characters involved.

Ghost In The Wires: My Adventures as the World's Most Wanted Hacker – Kevin Mitnick and William Simon

Acting as a biography of Mitnick's rise to infamy, this book depicts how he began his career of social engineering and code-cracking.

Cyber Wars – Charles Arthur
Former technology editor at *The Guardian*, Arthur's story of "game changing hacks that make organizations around the world tremble" was the second most-read on Perlego's cybersecurity list.

Automate the Boring Stuff with Python, 2nd Edition – Al Sweigart
The second most-read title on No Starch Press' cybersecurity list is another Python guide which promises to show the reader how to use Python to write programs in minutes with no prior programming experience required.

Secrets & Lies: Digital Security in a Networked World – Bruce Schneier
Schneier is a prolific writer and many recommendations were made for this 2000 title looking at the state of cybersecurity as we entered the new millennium.

Social Engineering – Christopher Hadnagy
Another with high Amazon ratings and recommended on Twitter, this 2010 book is widely recognized as the first to reveal the concept of social engineering.

Countdown to Zero Day – Kim Zetter
This book tells the tale of Stuxnet and the story of cyber-espionage involving the United States, Israel, and an Iranian nuclear facility.

The Code Book – The Science of Secrecy from Ancient Egypt to Quantum Cryptography by Simon Singh is a journey through time to look at the history of cryptography.

Ghosts in the Wires – My Adventures as the World's Most Wanted Hacker by Kevin Mitnick and William L. Simon (forward by Steve Wozniak) provides Mitnick's firsthand account of hacking.

Hacking: A Beginners' Guide To Computer Hacking, Basic Security, and Penetration Testing – by John Slavio is a practical handbook for people of all skill levels.

Hacking: The Art of Exploitation – by John Erickson explores how hacking techniques actually work.

Social Engineering: The Science of Human Hacking – by Christopher J. Hadnagy focuses on the motivations for hacking to help thwart future cybersecurity threats.

Permanent Record by Edward Snowden.

Countdown to Zero Day Stuxnet and the Launch of the World's First Digital Weapon by Kim Zetter.

Dark Territory The Secret History of Cyber War by Fred Kaplan.

Comptia Security + Get Certified Get Ahead Sy0-501 Study Guide by Darril Gibson.

The Art of Invisibility. The World's Most Famous Hacker Teaches You How to Be Safe in the Age of Big Brother and Big Data by Kevin Mitnick.

Ghost in the Wires. My Adventures as the World's Most Wanted Hacker by Kevin Mitnick, Steve Wozniak, William L. Simon.

The Cuckoo's Egg by Clifford Stoll.

Snow Crash by Neal Stephenson.

Sandworm. A New Era of Cyberwar and the Hunt for the Kremlin's Most Dangerous Hackers by Andy Greenberg.

Hacking The Art of Exploitation by Jon Erickson.

Kingpin. How One Hacker Took Over the Billion-Dollar Cybercrime Underground by Kevin Poulsen.

Future Crimes Everything Is Connected, Everyone Is Vulnerable, and What We Can Do About It by Marc Goodman.

The Code Book. The Science of Secrecy from Ancient Egypt to Quantum Cryptography by Simon Singh.

Spam Nation. The Inside Story of Organized Cybercrime-From Global Epidemic to Your Front Door by Brian Krebs.

Cyberwar. The Next Threat to National Security & What to Do About It by Richard A. Clarke, Robert Knake.

Practical Malware Analysis. The Hands-On Guide to Dissecting Malicious Software by Michael Sikorski.

The Perfect Weapon. War, Sabotage, and Fear in the Cyber Age by David E. Sanger.

Cybersecurity and Cyberwar. What Everyone Needs to Know by P.W. Singer and Allan Friedman.

Data and Goliath. The Hidden Battles to Collect Your Data and Control Your World by Bruce Schneier.

The Art of Deception. Controlling the Human Element of Security by Kevin D. Mitnick.

American Kingpin. The Epic Hunt for the Criminal Mastermind Behind the Silk Road by Nick Bilton.

Cryptonomicon by Neal Stephenson.

Red Team Field Manual (RTFM) by Ben Clark.

The Web Application Hacker's Handbook Finding and Exploiting Security Flaws by Dafydd Stuttard.

Social Engineering. The Science of Human Hacking by Hadnagy.

The Art of Intrusion. The Real Stories Behind the Exploits of Hackers, Intruders and Deceivers by Kevin D. Mitnick, William L. Simon.

Tribe of Hackers. Cybersecurity Advice from the Best Hackers in the World by Marcus J Carey, Jennifer Jin.

The Hacker Playbook 2. Practical Guide To Penetration Testing by Peter Kim.

The Phoenix Project. A Novel About IT, DevOps, and Helping Your Business Win by Gene Kim, Kevin Behr, George Spafford.

No Place to Hide. Edward Snowden, the NSA, and the US Surveillance State by Glenn Greenwald.

The Innovators. How a Group of Hackers, Geniuses and Geeks Created the Digital Revolution by Walter Isaacson.

We Are Anonymous. Inside the Hacker World of LulzSec, Anonymous, and the Global Cyber Insurgency by Parmy Olson.

Security Engineering. A Guide to Building Dependable Distributed Systems 2ed by Ross J. Anderson.

The Hacker Playbook 3. Practical Guide to Penetration Testing by Peter Kim.

Secrets and Lies. Digital Security in a Networked World by Bruce Schneier.

Black Hat Python. Python Programming for Hackers and Pentesters by Justin Seitz.

Click Here to Kill Everybody. Security and Survival in a Hyper-connected World by Bruce Schneier.

Applied Cryptography. Protocols, Algorithms, and Source Code in C by Bruce Schneier.

Mindf*ck. Cambridge Analytica and the Plot to Break America by Christopher Wylie.

The Age of Surveillance Capitalism. The Fight for a Human Future at the New Frontier of Power by Shoshana Zuboff.

Open Source Intelligence Techniques. Resources for Searching and Analyzing Online Information by Michael Bazzell.

Penetration Testing. A Hands-On Introduction to Hacking by Georgia Weidman.

The First Digital World War by Mark Bowden.

Cracking the Coding Interview. 189 Programming Questions and Solutions by Gayle Laakmann McDowell.

Lights Out: A Cyberattack: A Nation Unprepared. Surviving the Aftermath by Ted Koppel.

Hackers. Heroes of the Computer Revolution by Steven Levy.

Blue Team Field Manual (BTFM) by Alan J White.

Nmap Network Scanning. The Official Nmap Project Guide to Network Discovery and Security Scanning by Gordon Fyodor Lyon.

The Hacker Playbook. Practical Guide To Penetration Testing by Peter Ki.

@War. The Rise of the Military-Internet Complex by Shane Harris.

Malware Analyst's Cookbook and DVD. Tools and Techniques for Fighting Malicious Code by Michael Ligh, Steven Adair, Blake Hartstein, and Matthew Richard.

Metasploit. The Penetration Tester's Guide by David Kennedy, Jim O'Gorman, Devon Kearns, Mati Aharoni.

Threat Modeling Designing for Security by Adam Shostac.

Crypto. How the Code Rebels Beat the Government–Saving Privacy in the Digital Age by Steven Levy.

Automate the Boring Stuff with Python. Practical Programming for Total Beginners by Al Sweigart.

Gray Hat Hacking. The Ethical Hacker's Handbook by Allen Harper, Daniel Regalado et al.

Python Crash Course, 2nd Edition. A Hands-On, Project-Based Introduction to Programming by Eric Matthes.

Hacker, Hoaxer, Whistleblower, Spy. The Many Faces of Anonymous by Gabriella Coleman.

The Ultimate Unofficial Encyclopedia for Minecrafters. An A–Z Book of Tips and Tricks the Official Guides Don't Teach You by Megan Miller.

The Industries of the Future by Alec Ross.

The Basics of Hacking and Penetration Testing. Ethical Hacking and Penetration Testing Made Easy by Patrick Engebretson.

Cybersecurity: The Beginner's Guide. A comprehensive guide to getting started in cybersecurity by Dr. Erdal Ozkaya.

Cryptography Engineering. Design Principles and Practical Applications by Niels Ferguson, Bruce Schneier et al.

Windows Internals, Part 1 User Mode by Pavel Yosifovich, Mark E. Russinovich et al.

Comptia Network + Certification All-In-One Exam Guide, Seventh Edition (Exam N10-007) by Mike Meyers.

The Practice of Network Security Monitoring. Understanding Incident Detection and Response by Richard Bejtlich.

Wtf Is My Password. Password Book, Password Log Book and Internet Password Organizer, Alphabetical Password Book, Logbook to Protect Usernames and Passwords, Password Notebook, Password Book Small 6 × 9 by Booki Nova.

Minecraft. Guide to Creation by Mojang Ab.

The Hacked World Order. How Nations Fight, Trade, Maneuver, and Manipulate in the Digital Age by Adam Segal.

This Machine Kills Secrets. How WikiLeakers, Cypherpunks, and Hacktivists Aim to Free the World's Information by Andy Greenberg.

The Art of Memory Forensics. Detecting Malware and Threats in Windows, Linux, and Mac Memory by Michael Hale Ligh, Andrew Case, Jamie Levy, AAron Walters.

The IDA Pro Book. The Unofficial Guide to the World's Most Popular Disassembler by Chris Eagle 74.

The Fifth Domain. Defending Our Country, Our Companies, and Ourselves in the Age of Cyber Threats by Richard A. Clarke, Robert K. Knake.

Blue Team Handbook: Incident Response Edition. A condensed field guide for the Cyber Security Incident Responder by Don Murdoch GSE.

The Cybersecurity Dilemma. Network Intrusions, Trust, and Fear in the International System by Ben Buchanan.

The Hardware Hacker. Adventures in Making and Breaking Hardware by Andrew Bunnie Huang.

The Dark Net. Inside the Digital Underworld by Jamie Bartlett.

Violent Python. A Cookbook for Hackers, Forensic Analysts, Penetration Testers and Security Engineers by TJ O'Connor.

Cybersecurity Essentials by Charles J. Brooks, Christopher Grow et al.

Dark Mirror. Edward Snowden and the American Surveillance State by Barton Gellman.

CISSP All-in-One Exam Guide by Shon Harris.

How to Measure Anything in Cybersecurity Risk by Douglas W. Hubbard, Richard Seiersen, Daniel E. Geer Jr., Stuart McClure.

Password book: A Premium Journal and Logbook to Protect Usernames and Passwords Modern Password Keeper, Vault, Notebook and Online Organizer with … Calligraphy and Hand Lettering Design by Lettering Design Co.

Hacked Again by Scott N. Schober.

The Shellcoder's Handbook. Discovering and Exploiting Security Holes by Chris Anley, John Heasman, Felix Lindner, Gerardo Richarte.

Cybersecurity for Beginners by Raef Meeuwisse.

Cryptography Apocalypse. Preparing for the Day When Quantum Computing Breaks Today's Crypto by Roger A. Grimes.

Extreme Privacy. What It Takes to Disappear in America by Michael Bazzell.

Gray Day. My Undercover Mission to Expose America's First Cyber Spy by Eric O'Neill.

Minecraft. Guide to the Nether & the End by Mojang Ab.

Minecraft. Guide to Redstone by Mojang Ab.

McMafia. A Journey Through the Global Criminal Underworld by Misha Glenny.

CCNA 200-301 Official Cert Guide, Volume 1 by Wendell Odom.

(isc)2 Cissp Certified Information Systems Security Professional Official Study Guide, 8e & Cissp Official (Isc)2 Practice Tests, 2e by Mike Chapple.

Secrets of Reverse Engineering by Eldad Eilam.

Linux Basics for Hackers. Getting Started with Networking, Scripting, and Security in Kali by OccupyTheWeb.

Confront and Conceal. Obama's Secret Wars and Surprising Use of American Power by David E. Sange.

(isc)2 Cissp Certified Information Systems Security Professional Official Study Guide by Mike Chapple.

Cryptoconomy by Gary Miliefsky.

RESOURCES FOR HR DEPARTMENTS AND CYBERSECURITY JOB SEEKERS

https://infosec-jobs.com/
Find awesome jobs and talents in InfoSec/Cybersecurity

https://www.cyberseek.org/
Close the cybersecurity talent gap with interactive tools and data

https://cybersecjobs.com/
Information security jobs and career advice for cleared cybersecurity professionals

https://cybersn.com/
Your match awaits: The Cybersecurity Career Hub, matching talent to opportunity.

https://ninjajobs.org/
Trusted by the Top Brands: NinjaJobs has filled thousands of cybersecurity roles across numerous industries and well-known brands.

https://www.sans.org/hire-cyber-talent/
Hire Cyber Talent: Hire the right talent for the cyber roles on your team

https://www.cisa.gov/cyberjobs
Cybersecurity & IT Jobs at CISA: As technology becomes increasingly more sophisticated, the demand for an experienced and qualified cyber workforce to protect our Nation's networks and information systems has never been greater. Are you up for the challenge?

https://www.cybercom.mil/Employment-Opportunities/
We enable our most valuable assets – our people – in order to gain advantages in cyberspace

https://www.quitch.com/
Increase employee engagement and identify skill gaps in online learning and training instantly. As every moment your employee spends on training is time away from their jobs, gamifying training processes can help you reduce training costs.

https://www.shrm.org/resourcesandtools/pages/cybersecurity.aspx
With cyberthreats growing in sophistication, corporate digital security requires a real team effort. Employers can tap these resources for help improving their cybersecurity efforts in the workplace.

https://www.sans.org/blog/hr-cybersecurity/
SANS institute is committed to helping close the gap for top cybersecurity talent. Beyond training and certification, this gap also includes Human Resources and emerging talent learning how to enter the field successfully.

https://www.nist.gov/system/files/documents/2020/10/30/HR%20One%20Pager%20Final.pdf
Success Strategies for Cybersecurity Hiring for Human Resources and Hiring Professionals

https://www.isc2.org/#
(ISC)[2]: The World's Leading Cybersecurity Professional Organization

https://www.humanresourcestoday.com/cyber-security/
Cybersecurity or computer security and information security is the act of preventing theft, damage, loss, or unauthorized access to computers, networks, and data. Certifications for cybersecurity are hence the gateway toward pursuing this booming and unique professional space.

https://www.cybersafesolutions.com/
Cybersafe Solutions: The ultimate fusion of cutting-edge technology and human expertise.

https://isc2chapter-liny.org/
(ISC)² Long Island

https://coppertreestaffing.com/
Coppertree Staffing: From contract employees to full-time hires, we can help you succeed

https://www.forbes.com/sites/forbestechcouncil/2020/05/01/four-ways-employers-can-find-top-cybersecurity-talent/?sh=54854b6a768c
Four Ways Employers Can Find Top Cybersecurity Talent

https://www.betterteam.com/how-to-hire-information-security-analysts
How to Hire Information Security Analysts. A guide to help you recruit top information security analysts.

BIBLIOGRAPHY

A Frost & Sullivan Executive Briefing. (2017). *2017 global information security workforce study*. Retrieved from https://www.isc2.org/-/media/B7E003F79E1D4043A0E74A57D5B 6F33E.ashx

AICPA. (2017). *AICPA*. Retrieved from https://us.aicpa.org/ interestareas/frc/assuranceadvisoryservices/cyber-security-resource-center

Alguliyev, R., Imamverdiyev, Y., & Sukhostat, L. (2018). Cyber-physical systems and their security issues. *Computers in Industry*, *100*, 212–223.

Allison, L. (2016). You can't hack this: The regulatory future of cybersecurity in automobiles. *Journal Technology Law & Policy*, *21*, 15.

Ani, U. D., He, H., & Tiwari, A. (2019). Human factor security: Evaluating the cybersecurity capacity of the industrial workforce. *Journal of Systems and Information Technology*, *21*(1), 2–35.

Anwar, S., Mohamad Zain, J., Zolkipli, M. F., Inayat, Z., Khan, S., Anthony, B., & Chang, V. (2017). From intrusion detection to an intrusion response system: Fundamentals, requirements, and future directions. *Algorithms*, *10*(2), 39.

Arafah, M., Bakry, S. H., Al-Dayel, R., & Faheem, O. (2019, March). Exploring cybersecurity metrics for strategic units: A generic framework for future work. In *Future of information and communication conference* (pp. 881–891). Cham: Springer.

Arcuri, M. C., Gai, L., Ielasi, F., & Ventisette, E. (2020). Cyber attacks on hospitality sector: Stock market reaction. *Journal of Hospitality and Tourism Technology, 11*(2), 277–290.

Baden-Fuller, C., & Haefliger, S. (2013). Business models and technological innovation. *Long Range Planning, 46*(6), 419–426.

Bagchi-Sen, S., Rao, H. R., Upadhyaya, S. J., & Chai, S. (2010). Women in cybersecurity: A study of career advancement. *IT Professional, 12*(1), 24–31.

Barth, A., Jackson, C., & Mitchell, J. C. (2008). Robust defenses for cross-site request forgery. In *Proceedings of 15th ACM Conference*, CCS.

Beauchamp, C. L. (2022). *Exploring cyber ranges in cybersecurity education* (Doctoral dissertation, Virginia Tech).

Blair, J. R., Hall, A. O., & Sobiesk, E. (2019). Educating future multidisciplinary cybersecurity teams. *Computer, 52*(3), 58–66.

Bourgeois, D. T., Smith, J. L., Wang, S., & Mortati, J. (2019). *Information systems for business and beyond.*

Boyes, H. (2015). *Security, privacy, and the built environment* (Vol. 17, No. 3, pp. 25–31). IT Professional, Institute of Electrical and Electronics Engineers (IEEE).

Brayshaw, M., Gordon, N., & Karatazgianni, A. (2020). Identifying gaps in cybersecurity teaching and learning. *INSPIRE XXV*, 165.

Brenner, S. W. (2010). *Cybercrime: Criminal threats from cyberspace*. Santa Barbara, CA: ABC-CLIO.

Burley, D. (2021). The future of cyber: Educating the cybersecurity workforce (podcast series).

Burley, D. L., & McDuffie, E. L. (2015). An interview with Ernest McDuffie on the future of cybersecurity education. *ACM Inroads*, 6(2), 60–63.

Burris, J., Deneke, W., & Maulding, B. (2018, July). Activity simulation for experiential learning in cybersecurity workforce development. In *International Conference on HCI in Business, Government, and Organizations* (pp. 17–25). Springer, Cham.

Callahan, G., & Benzing, C. (2004). Assessing the role of internships in the career-oriented employment of graduating college students. *Education & Training*, 46(2), 82–89.

CAQ. (2018). *CAQ*. Retrieved from https://www.thecaq.org/cybersecurity-risk-management-oversight-tool-board-members/

Career Opportunities in the Internet of Things (IOT). (2021). *Futureoftech.org*. Retrieved from https://www.futureoftech.org/internet-of-things/6-career-opportunities-in-iot/

Chapple, M., Stewart, J. M., & Gibson, D. (2018). *(ISC) 2 CISSP certified information systems security professional official study guide*. Hoboken, NJ: John Wiley & Sons.

Chaudhary, H., Detroja, A., Prajapati, P., & Shah, P. (2020, December). A review of various challenges in cybersecurity using artificial intelligence. In *2020 3rd International Conference on Intelligent Sustainable Systems (ICISS)* (pp. 829–836). IEEE.

Cheng, X., & Walton, S. (2019). Do nonprofessional investors care about how and when data breaches are disclosed? *Journal of Information Systems*, *33*, 163–182. doi: 10.2308/isys-52410

Chudasama, D. (2021). Why choose cyber security as a career.

Coulton, P., Gradinar, A., & Lindley, J. (2021). Anticipating the adoption of IoT in everyday life.

Crumpler, W., & Lewis, J. A. (2019). *The cybersecurity workforce gap* (p. 10). Washington, DC: Center for Strategic and International Studies (CSIS).

Cyberspace solarium commission report. (2020). Retrieved from https://www.solarium.gov/report

D'Abate, C. (2010). Developmental interactions for business students: Do they make a difference? *Journal of Leadership & Organizational Studies*, *17*(2), 143–155.

Davies, G., Qasem, M., & Elmisery, A. M. (2020, December). Cyber security education and future provision. In *International Conference on Service-Oriented Computing* (pp. 612–626). Springer, Cham.

Dawson, J., & Thomson, R. (2018). The future cybersecurity workforce: Going beyond technical skills for successful cyber performance. *Frontiers in Psychology*, *9*, 744.

Deloitte. (2022). *Blockchain and quantum technologies: Driving the future of digital trust*. Retrieved from https://www2.deloitte.com/lu/en/pages/risk/articles/Blockchain-and-quantum-technologies-Driving-the-future-of-digital-trust.html

Dewar, R. S. (2014). *The "triptych of cyber security": A classification of active cyber defense.* Retrieved from https://www.academia.edu/6412868/_The_Triptych_of_Cyber_Security_A_Classification_of_Active_Cyber_Defence

Diogenes, Y., & Ozkaya, E. (2019). *Cybersecurity–Attack and defense strategies: Counter modern threats and employ state-of-the-art tools and techniques to protect your organization against cybercriminals.* Birmingham: Packt Publishing Ltd.

Dorsey, D. W., Martin, J., Howard, D. J., & Coovert, M. D. (2017). Cybersecurity issues in selection. In *Handbook of employee selection* (pp. 913–930).

Enoch, S. Y., Ge, M., Hong, J. B., & Kim, D. S. (2021). Model-based cybersecurity analysis: Past work and future directions. arXiv preprint arXiv:2105.08459.

Fafinski, S., Dutton, W. H., & Margetts, H. Z. (2010). *Mapping and measuring cybercrime.*

Finch, A., Burrell, D. N., Lu, S., Dawson, M., Springs, D., Bilberry, K., … Modeste, R. (2020). Cybersecurity workforce development in minority, low income, and native American reservation communities. *International Journal of Smart Education and Urban Society (IJSEUS), 11*(4), 35–52.

Fischer, E. A. (2014). *Federal laws relating to cybersecurity: Overview of major issues, current laws, and proposed legislation*: Congressional Research Service.

Fleishman, G. (2018). *Equifax data breach, one year later: Obvious errors and no real changes, new report says.* Retrieved from https://fortune.com/2018/09/07/equifax-data-breach-one-year-anniversary/

Gault, J., Redington, J., & Schlager, T. (2000). Undergraduate business internships and career success: Are they related? *Journal of Marketing Education, 22*(1), 45.

Geluvaraj, B., Satwik, P. M., & Ashok Kumar, T. A. (2019). The future of cybersecurity: Major role of artificial intelligence, machine learning, and deep learning in cyberspace. In *International conference on computer networks and communication technologies* (pp. 739–747). Singapore: Springer.

Geluvaraj, B., Satwik, P. M., & Kumar, T. A. (2019). The future of cybersecurity: Major role of artificial intelligence, machine learning, and deep learning in cyberspace. In *International Conference on Computer Networks and Communication Technologies* (pp. 739–747). Springer, Singapore.

Ghadiminia, N., Mayouf, M., Cox, S., & Krasniewicz, J. (2021). BIM-enabled facilities management (FM): A scrutiny of risks resulting from cyber attacks. *Journal of Facilities Management.*

Greenberg, A. (2018). *Marketing firm exactis leaked a personal info database with 340 million records.* Retrieved from https://www.wired.com/story/exactis-database-leak-340-million-records/

Greenfield, R. S. (2002). *Cyber forensics: A field manual for collecting, examining, and preserving evidence of computer crimes.* Auerbach Publications.

Haney, J. M., & Lutters, W. G. (2019, June). Motivating cybersecurity advocates: Implications for recruitment and retention. In Proceedings of the 2019 on *Computers and People Research Conference* (pp. 109–117).

Hargreaves, C., & Prince, D. (2013). Understanding cyber criminals and measuring their future activity.

Hargreaves, C., & Prince, D. D. (2013). Understanding cyber criminals and measuring their future activity developing cybercrime research. Security Lancaster. Lancaster University, Tech. Rep.

Hayes, A. (2023). *Blockchain facts: What is it, how it works, and how it can be used*. Retrieved from https://www. investopedia.com/terms/b/blockchain.asp

Hertzog, R., O'Gorman, J., & Aharoni, M. (2017). *Kali linux revealed. Mastering the penetration testing distribution*.

Hey, A. J., Tansley, S., Tolle, K. M., et al. (2009). *The fourth paradigm: Data-intensive scientific discovery* (Vol. 1). Redmond, WA: Microsoft Research.

Höhne, S., & Tiberius, V. (2020). Powered by blockchain: Forecasting blockchain use in the electricity market. *International Journal of Energy Sector Management, 14*(6), 1221–1238.

Hott, J. A., Stailey, D., Haderlie, D. M., & Ley, R. F. (2020). The CYBER security–competency health and maturity progression (CYBER-CHAMP) model: Extending the national initiative for cybersecurity education (NICE) framework across organizational security. *Cybersecurity Skills Journal: Practice and Research*. (INL/JOU-20-59690-Rev000).

Hott, J. A., Zohner, D. D., Fetzer, K. M., & Malzahn, T. E. (2019). Creating cybersecurity professionals of the future.

How to ace cybersecurity recruitment. (2022). Cybersn.com. Retrieved from https://cybersn.com/ace-cybersecurity-recruitment/

IBM security report. Retrieved from https://www.ibm.com/ security/data-breach

Igor, Z., Dmitry, M., Andrey, S., Dmitry, K., Anastasia, T., & Alexander, Z. (2013). Security software green head for mobile devices providing comprehensive protection from malware and illegal activities of cyber criminals. *International Journal of Computer Network and Information Security*, 5(5), 1–8.

Ikeda, K., Marshall, A., & Zaharchuk, D. (2019). Agility, skills and cybersecurity: Critical drivers of competitiveness in times of economic uncertainty. *Strategy & Leadership*, 47(3), 40–48.

ITU. (2008). *Committed to connecting the world*. Retrieved from https://www.itu.int/en/ITU-T/studygroups/com17/Pages/cybersecurity.aspx

Jahankhani, H., & Al-Nemrat, A. (2012). Examination of cyber-criminal behaviour. *International Journal of Information Science and Management (IJISM)*, 41–48.

Javed, A. R., Zikria, Y. B., Shahzad, F., & Jalil, Z. (2021). Future smart cities: Requirements, emerging technologies, applications, challenges, and future aspects. *Cities*, 129, 103794.

Jennifer, M., & Sandy, B. (2016). Trends in community colleges: Enrollment, prices, student debt, and completion. *College Board Research Brief*, 4, 1–23.

Jovanovic, V. M., Kuzlu, M., Popescu, O., Badawi, A. R., Marshall, D. K., Sarp, S., ... Wu, H. (2020). An initial look into the computer science and cybersecurity pathways project for career and technical education curricula.

Juniper Research. (2019). Retrieved from https://www.juniperresearch.com/

Kanellos. (2021). Cybersecurity challenges with emerging technologies. *JAPCC*. Retrieved from https://www.japcc.org/articles/cybersecurity-challenges-with-emerging-technologies/

Kaspersky. (2022). *What is the deep and dark web?* Retrieved from https://www.kaspersky.com/resource-center/threats/deep-web

Kerman, A., Borchert, O., & Rose, S. (2020). *Division, E. Tan, A.: Implementing a zero trust architecture, draft.* National Cyber Security Center of Excellence, National Institute of Standards and Technology, The Mitre Corporation. Retrieved from https://www.nccoe.nist.gov/sites/default/files/2022-12/zta-nist-sp-1800-35e-preliminary-draft.pdf

Kim, D. J., Love, B., & Kim, S. (2019). A comparison study of cybersecurity workforce frameworks and future directions. In *National cyber summit* (pp. 85–96).

Kirvan, P., & Granneman, J. (2022). Top 10 IT security frameworks and standards explained. Techtarget.com. Retrieved from https://www.techtarget.com/searchsecurity/tip/IT-security-frameworks-and-standards-Choosing-the-right-one

Knaves, M. (2022). Cybersecurity risk management: Frameworks, plans, & best practices.

Knouse, S. B., & Fontenot, G. (2008). Benefits of the business college internship: A research review. *Journal of Employment Counseling, 45*(2), 61–66.

Knouse, S., Tanner, J., & Harris, E. (1999). The relation of college internships, college performance, and subsequent job opportunity. *Journal of Employment Counseling, 36*(1), 35–43.

Koch, R. (2017). On the future of cybersecurity. In *ICMLG 2017 5th International Conference on Management Leadership and Governance* (p. 202). Academic Conferences and Publishing Limited.

Kuerbis, B., & Badiei, F. (2017). Mapping the cybersecurity institutional landscape. In *Digital policy, regulation and governance*.

Kumar, S., Velliangiri, S., Karthikeyan, P., Kumari, S., Kumar, S., & Khan, M. K. (2021). A survey on the blockchain techniques for the Internet of Vehicles security. *Transactions on Emerging Telecommunications Technologies*, e4317.

Kwan, L., Ray, P., & Stephens, G. (2008, January). Towards a methodology for profiling cyber criminals. In *Proceedings of the 41st Annual Hawaii International Conference on System Sciences (HICSS 2008)*. IEEE (p. 264).

Lachow, I. (2011). The Stuxnet enigma: Implications for the future of cybersecurity. *Georgetown Journal of International Affairs*, 118–126.

Landwehr, C. (2008, September/October). Cybersecurity and artificial intelligence: From fixing the plumbing to smart water. In *IEEE, Security and privacy* (p. 3).

Lapena, R. (2017). *Survey says: Soft skills highly valued by security team*. Retrieved from https://www.tripwire.com/state-of-security/featured/survey-says-soft-skills-highly-valued-security-team/

Li, Z. (2020). Seven cybersecurity considerations. In *Routledge handbook of international cybersecurity*.

Liu, F., & Tu, M. (2020). An analysis framework of portable and measurable higher education for future cybersecurity workforce development. *Journal of Education and Learning (EduLearn)*, 14(3), 322–330.

Martellini, M., Abaimov, S., Gaycken, S., & Wilson, C. (2017). Future attack patterns. In *Information security of highly critical wireless networks* (pp. 59–62). Cham: Springer.

Mathew, A. (2021). Artificial intelligence for offence and defense-the future of cybersecurity. *Educational Research*, *3*(3), 159–163.

Maughan, D., Balenson, D., Lindqvist, U., & Tudor, Z. (2015). Government-funded R&D to drive cybersecurity technologies. *IT Professional*, *17*(4), 62–65.

McBride, S., Schou, C., & Slay, J. An initial industrial cybersecurity workforce development framework.

McDonough, B. R. (2018). *Cyber smart: Five habits to protect your family, money, and identity from cyber criminals*. Hoboken, NJ: John Wiley & Sons.

McDuffie, E. L., & Piotrowski, V. P. (2014). The future of cybersecurity education. *IEEE Annals of the History of Computing*, *47*(08), 67–69.

McQuaid, P. A., & Cervantes, S. (2019). How to achieve a seasoned cybersecurity workforce. *Software Quality Professional*, *21*(4).

Milošević, Đ. M. (2022). Frequent occurring forms of internet frauds. *Baština*, (56), 209–227.

Miranda-Calle, J. D., Reddy, V., Dhawan, P., & Churi, P. (2021). Exploratory data analysis for cybersecurity. *World Journal of Engineering*, *18*(5), 734–749.

Molloy, I., Rao, J. R., & Stoecklin, M. P. (2021, April). AI vs. AI: Exploring the intersections of AI and cybersecurity. In *Proceedings of the 2021 ACM Workshop on Security and Privacy Analytics* (p. 1).

Momani, A. M., & Jamous, M. (2017). The evolution of technology acceptance theories. *International Journal of Contemporary Computer Research (IJCCR)*, *1*(1), 51–58.

Morel, B. (2011, October). Artificial intelligence and the future of cybersecurity. In *Proceedings of the 4th ACM workshop on Security and artificial intelligence* (pp. 93–98).

Morgan, S. (2015). *Cybersecurity market reaches $75 billion in 2015; Expected to reach $170 billion by 2020.* Retrieved from https://www.forbes.com/sites/stevemorgan/2015/12/20/cybersecurity%E2%80%8B-%E2%80%8Bmarket-reaches-75-billion-in-2015%E2%80%8B%E2%80%8B-%E2%80%8Bexpected-to-reach-170-billion-by-2020/?sh=16f0a0ba30d6

Mpuru, L., & Kgoale, C. (2019). Cybercrime-biggest cyberthreats in future? *Servamus Community-based Safety and Security Magazine*, 112(10), 22–23.

Murray, G., Johnstone, M. N., & Valli, C. (2017). *The convergence of IT and OT in critical infrastructure.*

Nakamoto, S. (2008). *Bitcoin whitepaper.* Retrieved from https://bitcoin.org/bitcoin.pdf. Accessed on July 17, 2019.

Nelson, R. R. (1994). The co-evolution of technology, industrial structure, and supporting institutions. *Industrial and Corporate Change*, 3(1), 47–63.

Newhouse, W., et al. (2017). National initiative for cybersecurity education (NICE) cybersecurity workforce framework. NIST Special Publication 800.2017 (2017), 181.

Newhouse, B., Keith, S., Scribner, B., & Witte, G. (2016). Nice cybersecurity workforce framework (ncwf). Draft NIST Special Publication 800, 181, 800-181.

Nye, J. (2018). *How will new cybersecurity norms develop?*, Project Syndicate.

Oxford Analytica. Connected cars have a large cybersecurity risk surface. Emerald Expert Briefings (oxan-db).

Oxford Analytica. Prospects for cybersecurity to end-2020. Emerald Expert Briefings (oxan-db).

Oxford Analytica. (2016). Cybercrime is set for global growth. Emerald Expert Briefings (oxan-db).

Peng, Y., Lu, T., Liu, J., Gao, Y., Guo, X., & Xie, F. (2013). Cyber-physical system risk assessment. In *Proceedings - 2013 9th International Conference on Intelligent Information Hiding and Multimedia Signal Processing*, IIH-MSP 2013. doi:10.1109/IIH-MSP.2013.116

Perry, A. M. (2019). *Black workers are being left behind by full employment*. Retrieved from https://www.brookings.edu/blog/the-avenue/2019/06/26/black-workers-are-being-left-behind-by-full-employment/

Ponemon. (2019). *Cost of a data breach report*. Retrieved from https://www.ibm.com/downloads/cas/RDEQK07R

Quade, P. (2019). *The digital big bang: The hard stuff, the soft stuff, and the future of cybersecurity*.

Rai, M., & Mandoria, H. (2019). A study on cyber crimes cyber criminals and major security breaches. *International Research Journal of Engineering Technology*, 6(7), 1–8.

Raj, R. K., Ekstrom, J. J., Impagliazzo, J., Lingafelt, S., Parrish, A., Reif, H., & Sobiesk, E. (2017, October). Perspectives on the future of cybersecurity education. In *2017 IEEE Frontiers in Education Conference (FIE)* (pp. 1–2). IEEE.

Ray, L. (2017). Survey says: Soft skills highly valued by security team. Retrieved from https://www.tripwire.com/state-of-security/featured/survey-says-soft-skills-highly-valued-security-team/

Richet, J. L. (2013). From young hackers to crackers. *International Journal of Technology and Human Interaction (IJTHI)*, 9(3), 53–62.

Richet, J. L. (2015). How to become a cybercriminal?: An explanation of cybercrime diffusion. In *Human behavior, psychology, and social interaction in the digital era* (pp. 229–240).

Rogers, K. (2019, November 1). Jobs: Companies struggle to find skilled cybersecurity workers as attacks intensify. Retrieved from https://www.cnbc.com/2019/11/01/jobs-companies-need-cybersecurity-workers-asattacks-intensify.html

Roohani, S. J., & Zheng, X. (2019). Using ten teaching modules and recently publicized data-breach cases to integrate cybersecurity into upper-level accounting courses. In *Advances in accounting education: Teaching and curriculum innovations*. Bingley: Emerald Publishing Limited.

Rose, L. A. (2021). Bridging the realms between cyber and physical: Approaching cyberspace with an interdisciplinary lens.

Sabillon, R., Cavaller, V., Cano, J., & Serra-Ruiz, J. (2016, June). Cybercriminals, cyberattacks and cybercrime. In *2016 IEEE International Conference on Cybercrime and Computer Forensic (ICCCF)* (pp. 1–9). IEEE.

Saleem, J., Islam, R., & Kabir, M. A. (2022). The anonymity of the dark web: A survey. *IEEE Access*, 10, 33628–33660.

Sarker, I. H., Kayes, A. S. M., Badsha, S., Alqahtani, H., Watters, P., & Ng, A. (2020). Cybersecurity data science: An overview from machine learning perspective. *Journal of Big Data*, 7(1), 1–29.

Savino, J. O., & Turvey, B. E. (Eds.). (2011). *Rape investigation handbook*. Academic Press.

Schehl, M. (2019). NPS intern prepares to take on next-gen cybercriminals.

Schiks, J. A., van de Weijer, S. G., & Leukfeldt, E. R. (2022). High tech crime, high intellectual crime? Comparing the intellectual capabilities of cybercriminals, traditional criminals and non-criminals. *Computers in Human Behavior, 126,* 106985.

Seals, B. (2019). PELP fall speaker series addresses the future of cybersecurity.

Segal, A., Akimenko, V., Giles, K., Pinkston, D. A., Lewis, J. A., Bartlett, B., ... Noor, E. (2020). The future of cybersecurity across the Asia-Pacific. *Asia Policy, 15*(2), 57–59.

Sharma, A. C., Gandhi, R. A., Mahoney, W., Sousan, W., & Zhu, Q. (2010, August). Building a social dimensional threat model from current and historic events of cyber attacks. In *2010 IEEE Second International Conference on Social Computing* (pp. 981-986). IEEE.

Sharma, R., & Mishra, R. (2014). A review of evolution of theories and models of technology adoption. *Indore Management Journal, 6*(2), 17–29.

Sharp Sr, W. G. (2010). The past, present, and future of cybersecurity. *Journal of National Security Law & Policy, 4,* 13.

Silverstein, J. (2019). *Hundreds of millions of Facebook user records were exposed on Amazon cloud server*. Retrieved from https://www.cbsnews.com/news/millions-facebook-user-records-exposed-amazon-cloud-server/

Singapore's Cybersecurity Strategy. (2016). CSA Singapore, 10 October. Retrieved from www.csa.gov.sg/news/ publications/singapore-cybersecurity-strategy

Skertic, J. (2021). Cybersecurity legislation and ransomware attacks in the United States, 2015–2019.

Smith, Z. M., Lostri, E., & Lewis, J. A. (2020). The hidden costs of Cybercrime. McAfee. Retrieved from https://www. mcafee.com/enterprise/en-us/assets/reports/rp-hidden-costs-ofcybercrime.pdf

Sobel, A., Parrish, A., & Raj, R. K. (2019). Curricular foundations for cybersecurity. *Computer*, *52*(3), 14–17.

Sommer, P., & Brown, I. (2011, January 14). *Reducing systemic cybersecurity risk*. Organisation for Economic Cooperation and Development Working Paper No. IFP/WKP/ FGS(2011)3. Available at SSRN; Retrieved from https://ssrn. com/abstract=1743384

Souppaya, M., Scarfone, K., & Dodson, D. (2021). Secure software development framework (SSDF) Version 1.1: Recommendations for mitigating the risk of software vulnerabilities (No. NIST Special Publication (SP) 800-218 (Draft)). National Institute of Standards and Technology.

Stempfley, B. (2019). *The future of cybersecurity*. Pittsburgh PA: Carnegie Mellon University.

Sukhai, N. B. (2004, October). Hacking and cybercrime. In *Proceedings of the 1st annual conference on Information security curriculum development* (pp. 128–132).

Sulek, D., Moran, N., & Principal, B. A. H. (2009). What analogies can tell us about the future of cybersecurity. In *The virtual battlefield: Perspectives on cyber warfare* (Vol. 3, pp. 118–131).

Summit, H. B. C. U., Platform, N. L., Polls, N. Q., Briefs, N. A. C. E., & Market, J. (2017). The positive implications of internships on early career outcomes. *NACE Journal*.

Szyliowicz, J. S., & Zamparini, L. (2014). *Maritime security: Issues and challenges. Maritime transport security*, 13–23.

Tao, F., Akhtar, M. S., & Jiayuan, Z. (2021). The future of artificial intelligence in cybersecurity: A comprehensive survey. *EAI Endorsed Transactions on Creative Technologies*, *8*(28), e3–e3.

Terry, I. (2017). The future of cybersecurity regulations: 2017 New York DFS changes.

10 Skills and attributes of a successful cybersecurity pro. (2021). Terranovasecuirty.com. Retrieved from https://terranovasecurity.com/10-attributes-of-a-natural-born-cyber-security-professional/

Top 11 Most Powerful CyberSecurity Software Tools In 2022. (2022, July). Softwaretestinghelp.com. Retrieved from https://www.softwaretestinghelp.com/cybersecurity-software-tools/

Vaishy, S., & Gupta, H. (2021, September). Cybercriminals' motivations for targeting government organizations. In *2021 9th International Conference on Reliability, Infocom Technologies and Optimization (Trends and Future Directions) (ICRITO)* (pp. 1–6). IEEE.

Van Hardeveld, G. J., Webber, C., & O'Hara, K. (2017). Deviating from the cybercriminal script: Exploring tools of anonymity (mis) used by carders on cryptomarkets. *American Behavioral Scientist*, *61*(11), 1244–1266.

Von Solms, R., & Van Niekerk, J. (2013). From information security to cyber security. *Computers & Security*, *38*, 97–102. doi:10.1016/j.cose.2013.04.004

Wall, D. (2007). *Cybercrime: The transformation of crime in the information age* (Vol. 4). Polity.

Walton, S., Wheeler, P. R., Zhang, Y., & Zhao, X. (2021). An integrative review and analysis of cybersecurity research: Current state and future directions. *Journal of Information Systems, 35*(1), 155–186.

Wang, P., & Sbeit, R. (2020). A comprehensive mentoring model for cybersecurity education. In *17th International Conference on Information Technology–New Generations (ITNG 2020)* (pp. 17–23). Springer, Cham.

Waters, J. (2020). 5G 101 guide: What it is and what it's not (and why). *Future Tech 360*. Retrieved from https://futuretech360.com/articles/2020/04/14/5g-101-guide.aspx

Watters, P. A., McCombie, S., Layton, R., & Pieprzyk, J. (2012). Characterising and predicting cyber attacks using the cyber attacker model profile (CAMP). *Journal of Money Laundering Control, 15*(4), 430–441.

What is quantum computing? (2021). IBM.com. Retrieved from https://www.ibm.com/topics/quantum-computing

What is the deep and dark web? (2022). *Kasperky.com*. Retrieved from https://www.kaspersky.com/resource-center/threats/deep-web

What is Hardware and Software Security? (2022, June). *Wheelhouse.com*. Retrieved from https://www.wheelhouse.com/resources/what-is-hardware-and-software-security-a11018#gref

What is the Internet of Vehicles (IoV). (2022). *EasternPeak.com*. Retrieved from https://easternpeak.com/definition/internet-of-vehicles-iov/

What is IOT. (2022). *Oracle.com*. Retrieved from https://www.oracle.com/internet-of-things/what-is-iot/

What's the role of HR in cybersecurity and why is it important. (2021). *You.com*. Retrieved from https://www.yoh.com/blog/whats-the-role-of-hr-in-cybersecurity-and-why-is-it-important

What is a Zero Trust Architecture. (2021). *PaloAltoNetworks.com*. Retrieved from https://www.paloaltonetworks.com/cyberpedia/what-is-a-zero-trust-architecture

Willison, R. (2006). Understanding the perpetration of employee computer crime in the organisational context. *Information and organization*, 16(4), 304–324.

Wood, B. J. (2000). *An insider threat model for adversary simulation*. Albuquerque: SRI International, Cyber Defense Research Center. System Design Laboratory.

Yadav, K., Sethi, A., Kaur, M., & Perakovic, D. (2022). Machine learning for malware analysis: Methods, challenges, and future directions. In *Advances in malware and data-driven network security* (pp. 1–18). Hershey, PA: IGI Global.

Yampolskiy, R. V. (2019). Predicting future AI failures from historic examples. *Foresight*.

Yar, M. (2005). The novelty of 'Cybercrime' an assessment in light of routine activity theory. *European Journal of Criminology*, 2(4), 407–427.

Yusuf Enoch, S., Ge, M., Hong, J. B., & Kim, D. S. (2021). Model-based cybersecurity analysis: Past work and future directions. arXiv e-prints arXiv-2105.

Yu, S., Zhou, W., Dou, W., & Makki, S. K. (2012, June). Why it is hard to fight against cyber criminals? In *2012 32nd International Conference on Distributed Computing Systems Workshops* (pp. 537–541). IEEE.

INDEX